CORUNNA

D1637771

THE AUTHOR

Christopher Hibbert was born in Leicestershire in 1924 and educated at Radley and Oriel College, Oxford. He served as an infantry officer during the war, was twice wounded and was awarded the Military Cross in 1945. Described by Professor J. H. Plumb as 'a writer of the highest ability' and in the *New Statesman* as 'a pearl of biographers', he is, in the words of *The Times Educational Supplement*, 'perhaps the most gifted popular historian we have'. His much acclaimed books include the following, *The Destruction of Lord Raglan* (which won the Heinemann Award for Literature in 1962); *Benito Mussolini; The Court at Windsor; The Making of Charles Dickens; London: The Biography of a City; The Dragon Wakes: China and the West 1793–1911; George IV; The Rise and Fall of the House of Medici; Edward VII: A Portrait; The Great Mutiny: India 1857; The French Revolution; The Personal History of Samuel Johnson; Africa Explored; Garibaldi and His Enemies; Rome: The Biography of a City; The Virgin Queen: The Personal History of Elizabeth I; Florence: The Biography of a City; and Nelson: A Personal History.*

Christopher Hibbert is a Fellow of the Royal Society of Literature. He is married with two sons and a daughter and lives in Henley-on-Thames.

CORUNNA

CHRISTOPHER HIBBERT

THE WINDRUSH PRESS · GLOUCESTERSHIRE

First published in Great Britain by
B.T. Batsford Ltd, 1961
Reprinted by The Windrush Press, 1996
Little Window, High Street,
Moreton-in-Marsh
Gloucestershire GL56 0LL
Telephone: 01608 652012
Fax: 01608 652125

British Library Cataloguing in Publication Data
A catalogue record for this book is available from the British Library

ISBN 0 900075 84 8

Typeset by Archetype, Stow-on-the-Wold
Printed and bound in Great Britain by Bell & Bain Ltd., Glasgow

The front cover shows a detail from an aquatint by
T. Sutherland of the death of Sir John Moore. Reproduced
by courtesy of The Mary Evans Picture Library

For Judy

Contents

PART ONE: *Lisbon*

PART TWO: *The Advance*

PART THREE: *The Retreat*

PART FOUR: *Corunna*

Preface

One of the best remembered poems in the English language has served to keep alive the memory of Sir John Moore and of his burial at Corunna on 17th January, 1809. The story of the battle which he fought on the previous day and of the short campaign and horrifying retreat which preceded it is not, of course, so well known. A book specifically devoted to these events has not been written before, although numerous biographies, histories of the Peninsular War, diaries, memoirs, letters and regimental histories have made them familiar in a general way.

For their help in finding the various authorities on which I have based my book I am grateful to Mr. D. W. King, the War Office Librarian and his staff; Brigadier John Stephenson and the librarian's staff at the Royal United Service Institution; Miss Susanna Fisher of the manuscript department of the National Maritime Museum; and the staffs of the British Museum, the Public Record Office, the London Library and the Codrington Library. A note on these authorities and a list of them will be found at the end of the book.

I want also to thank Miss Frances Ryan for helping me in my researches, and Major Freddie Myatt for helping me with the maps and appendices and for having read the proofs.

CHRISTOPHER HIBBERT

Illustrations

'The Convention of Cintra, a Portuguese Gambol for the
Amusement of John Bull' engraved from a drawing by
G. Woodward, 1809
by courtesy of the Trustees of the British Museum

Soldiers on the March from a caricature by
Thomas Rowlandson
by courtesy of the Trustees of the British Museum

Plate Section between pages 114 and 115

The brigades under Major-General Fraser crossing the River
Tagus near Villa Velha from an aquatint after an eye-witness
sketch by the Rev. William Bradford
by courtesy of the Trustees of the British Museum

A snow-covered pass in Galicia from a sketch by Sir Robert
Ker Porter
by courtesy of the Trustees of the British Museum

The road to Corunna from a sketch by Sir Robert Ker Porter
by courtesy of the Trustees of the British Museum

Corunna Harbour at the time of the explosion on
13 January 1809 from a sketch by Sir Robert Ker Porter
by courtesy of the Trustees of the British Museum

View of Corunna during the battle by H. Lecomte
Hulton Deutsch Collection

Battle of Corunna, 16 January 1809 from an aquatint by
M. Duborg, after a contemporary drawing by W. Heath
Hulton Deutsch Collection

The Burial of Sir John Moore
Hulton Deutsch Collection

MAPS

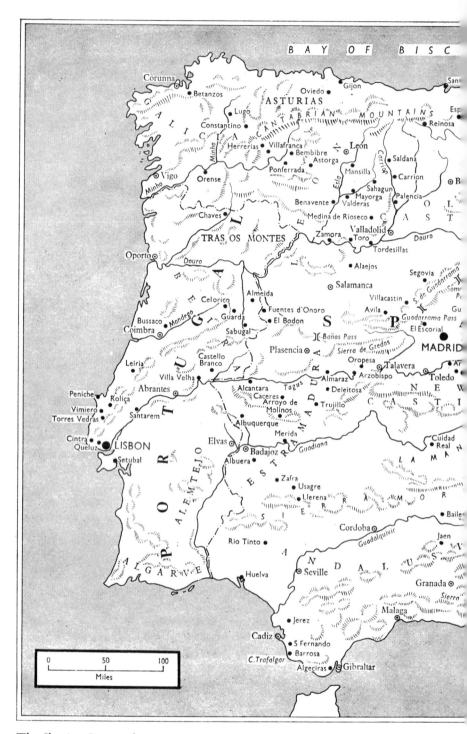

The Iberian Peninsular

PART ONE

Lisbon

1

Beginning of the War

'The English declare they will no longer respect neutrals on the sea; I will
no longer recognise them on land.'

Napoleon Buonaparte

IT WAS insufferably hot. For five days now the landing craft, packed with
soldiers sitting four by four on the thwarts, had been plunging violently
through the Atlantic breakers towards the burning sand of the beach.
There had been a storm the first night, but the water had soon soaked away
and the shore, dried by the fierce and constant sunlight, was parched again.

Groups of thirsty sailors, the white surf frothing round their thighs,
stood naked at the water's edge, watching the heavily loaded boats sweep
forward through the spray. In the instant that the waters rushed back
under the foam of a broken wave, the sailors ran out towards the boats
to hurl a rope towards them. More often than not the end of the rope
fell short into the water or sometimes a sailor lost his balance in the
swirling currents and was caught up and swept back by the next great roll
of the sea. Sitting with their packs and muskets held tightly between their
knees, the soldiers waited nervously for the jerk that would tell them that
the rope had been caught and the slack taken in, and then the boat would
go scudding over the shallow water to the safety of the beach.

Above the high-water mark immense piles of food and ammunition,
equipment and forage lay waiting for transport to take them inland. A
harassed German commissary, scribbling an inventory in his notebook,
looked in consternation at the guns and wagons, 'the mountains of ship's
biscuit, haversacks, trusses of hay, barrels of meat and rum, tents' and all
the impedimenta needed by a British army of 13,000 men. Around him
officers shouting orders, sergeants sweating and cursing, soldiers picking
up the wreckage of splintered boats, aides-de-camp and orderlies
choosing sites for the generals' tents moved about barefoot up and down
the beach and sometimes went to paddle in the surf to cool themselves.
Frightened horses, released from weeks of confinement in the dark and
stuffy holds of ships, galloped wildly along the shore, snorting, panting,
neighing, biting one another, and rolling over in the sand, while dragoons

chased after them, bridles in hand. Many of the horses had lost the strength of their legs from having been kept standing in the ships for so long, and the moment a trooper saddled and mounted one of them the poor animal's hind quarters drooped absurdly to the ground.

Winding their way through the noise and muddle, brown-skinned peasants, their long black hair falling to their shoulders beneath enormous three cornered hats, led bullock carts which screeched so fearfully above the roar of the surf that the scratching of a knife on a pewter plate seemed like 'the sweet sound of a flute beside them'. Regardless of the heat they wore thick blankets or large brown cloaks over their shoulders, and every now and then they goaded their mournful bullocks by striking them over the back with pikes six feet long. Watched by scores of monks and friars, each of whom carried a vast and luridly coloured umbrella, the peasants offered pumpkins and figs, grapes and melons, wine and apples for sale to the dry-throated troops.

It was 7th August 1808 and the British army was landing on the coast of Napoleon's Europe, a hundred miles north of Lisbon. The year before a previous landing on the shores of the hostile continent had been made at Vedboek. The troops had rushed through the pinewoods to Copenhagen and on September 7th, after three days' heavy bombardment of their beautiful capital, the Danes surrendered. The Danish fleet, which it was feared would fall into Napoleon's hands, was removed from under his nose. The Emperor was furious. He renewed his threats of invasion; he told Talleyrand that all the ports of Europe, neutral or not, would soon have to be closed to English ships; that every English Minister on the Continent would have to be sent home; that all individual Englishmen must be arrested. He lost his temper with the representative of England's oldest ally at a reception and shouted at him:

> If Portugal does not do what I want, the House of Braganza will not be reigning in Europe in two months. I will no longer tolerate an English ambassador in Europe.... The English declare they will no longer respect neutrals on the sea; I will no longer recognise them on land!

Within a few days the French Ambassador had left Lisbon, and a French army of 30,000 men was being concentrated under General Junot at Bayonne. The march through Spain would present no problems as, despite murmurs of discontent and occasional displays of independence, Manuel de Godoy, the Spanish dictator and his Queen's lover, was little more than Napoleon's puppet. On 30th November, 1807, after moving across Spain at an astonishing speed, the vanguard of

Junot's army marched into the streets of Lisbon. The day before Prince John, the Regent of Portugal, escorted by British warships had sailed for Rio de Janeiro. The *Moniteur* announced that the House of Braganza, as the Emperor had promised, was in fact no longer reigning in Europe.

It was all part of a larger design. Napoleon's economic war would never be successful while the Royal Navy was able to pass unchallenged through the seaways of the world. His blockade hurt Britain, but it could not starve her. The British command of the sea must, therefore, be broken. The Mediterranean must be conquered. Three attacks were envisaged. One in the eastern Mediterranean through the Turkish Empire as a threat to India; one in the central Mediterranean against Sicily; the third, and most forceful, in the western Mediterranean through Spain to Gibraltar and the coasts of North Africa.

The plans for this, the crucial attack, were carefully laid. By threats and promises Godoy was made more afraid of Napoleon and more dependent upon him than he had ever been; by the Machiavellian use of some indiscreet letters to the Emperor, which Prince Ferdinand, the dissolute but not unpopular heir to the Spanish throne, had written, the King of Spain, Charles IV, was induced to have his son arrested for treason; and, by the skilful manipulation of a minor revolution which this arrest provoked, the King was persuaded to abdicate in favour of Ferdinand. The deposed King and Queen tried to make their escape to South America, but the mob prevented them; and Napoleon then had no difficulty in luring them to Bayonne where Godoy joined them. Prince Ferdinand was also induced by the Emperor to cross over into France where he was confronted by his angry parents, who told him he was a bastard. Neither an ambitious nor a strong-willed man, the Prince, in return for a pension, agreed to execute with the King and Queen an abdication of the throne which was immediately offered to Joseph Buonaparte by a few compliant Spanish Grandees.

While quickly settling the political fate of the Spanish royal family, Napoleon had meanwhile been strengthening his military hold on their country. By the secret Treaty of Fontainebleau, signed on 27th October, 1807, he had already secured Spanish assistance in the attack on Portugal and authority to occupy several large towns south of the Pyrenees. Three months later even the pretence of formally negotiated settlements was given up, and French troops poured into Spain as an undisguised occupation force. It was a familiar Napoleonic pattern, but it had an unfamiliar result. It had not been difficult to do away with the feeble Spanish Bourbons. '*Un Bourbon sur le trône d'Espagne c'est un voisin trop dangereux*', he had said, having no doubt that he could push Charles IV off the throne as easily as he could push the representative of the House of Braganza off the throne of Portugal.

But Napoleon's calculations had not allowed for the patriotism, the courage and the pride of the Spanish people. On 2nd May, 1808, the people of Madrid turned furiously on the French garrison and shot and stabbed every soldier they could find. And although the revolt was soon put down by the ruthless fire of French guns, which by nightfall had filled the streets with blood, less than three weeks later the anger broke out again in other towns, in other provinces. Spanish officials who had shown themselves corruptible by French money or the offer of power were dragged out into the streets and murdered. In Badajoz, in Cartagena, in Jaen and in Cadiz, governors and *Corregidores* were lynched by the mob. In Valencia, in the Asturias and in Andalusia, committees were organised, troops were enrolled, proclamations promising support to Prince Ferdinand and death to the French were read to wildly cheering crowds.

At the end of May General Sir Hew Dalrymple, Governor of Gibraltar, forwarded to London a request he had received from the Junta of Seville for money and arms. A week later six representatives of the Asturian Juntas landed at Falmouth with a fervent appeal for help from a country with which Spain was still officially at war. They were welcomed sympathetically. Past quarrels were forgotten. George Canning, the Foreign Secretary and most influential member of the old Duke of Portland's Administration, announced that 'Britain would proceed upon the principle that any nation of Europe which starts up with a determination to oppose a Power which, whether professing insidious peace or declaring open war, is the common enemy of all nations, becomes instantly our ally'. In replying to this announcement for the Opposition, Richard Brinsley Sheridan showed that the country was united in its enthusiasm for the Spanish cause. 'Hitherto ', he said in a speech which brought tears to the eyes of Members on both sides of the House,

> Buonaparte has had to contend against princes without dignity and ministers without wisdom. He has fought against countries in which people have been indifferent to his success; he has yet to learn what it is to fight against a country in which the people are animated with one spirit to resist him.

Never, he thought, had there been 'anything so brave, so generous, so noble' as the conduct of the Spanish patriots.

No one could doubt the importance of their resistance. At last there had come an opportunity to build up a dam against the flood tide of Napoleon's success. The nationalist reaction had begun; and, if the spark caught flame and the flames were fanned and spread, all Europe might be caught up in the fire. Were help to be given promptly the first step would be taken towards what Sheridan called in a dramatic phrase, 'the emancipation of the world'.

Help *was* given promptly. Peace was declared and an alliance pronounced. At the War Office Lord Castlereagh considered a report from Lieutenant-General Sir Arthur Wellesley who suggested that 'this would appear to be a crisis in which a great effort might be made with advantage; and it is certain that any measures which can distress the French in Spain must oblige them to delay for a season' the execution of their other plans. Sir Arthur had under his command at Cork rather more than 9,000 troops which it had been intended to send to Venezuela in the hope of bringing about a revolution there. There were 5,000 more men in transports at Gibraltar, where they had been sent after the failure of General Whitelocke's attempt to set free the Spanish colonies and open up their trade to British ships. Major-General William Carr Beresford had 3,000 more at Madeira, which had been occupied the previous December in the name of the exiled Prince John of Portugal. There were 10,000 men off the Swedish coast under Sir John Moore whose views on the uses to which they could usefully be put were not those of the mad King of Sweden, who would only let the English troops land if they helped him defy the threatening armies of France, Russia and Denmark in a wild attempt to recover Pomerania and Finland. In all there were then over 27,000 men available for a continental invasion. It was certainly a small enough number compared with the 100,000 troops which Napoleon had already sent into Spain; but it was a far larger one than the Horse Guards could usually be expected to concentrate at short notice for an operation in Europe.

Towards the end of June the Government were given further encouragement when the spirit of resistance in Spain spread to Portugal. It was decided before the month was over to send Sir Arthur Wellesley, with the troops at Cork and 4,000 of the men from Gibraltar, to the help of the Spaniards by making a diversionary attack on Junot's forces in Portugal. Thus it was that two months after the envoys from the Asturias had landed in England, 13,000 British troops were disembarking on the long and sandy beaches of Mondego Bay and preparing to march south against the unknown strength of the French army.

On 9th August, 1808, Sir Arthur Wellesley was riding down the road to Leiria. One of his aides-de-camp noticed how disconsolate he looked. He had reason to be. At Mondego Bay he had been handed despatches from London. They contained distasteful news. Some members of the Government, and Castlereagh in particular, had done their best for him;

but the objections of other Ministers and the senior officers of the Horse
Guards had in the end prevailed. The newly created lieutenant-general
was not yet forty. There were numerous other names in the Army list
more senior to his. Both the King and his son the Duke of York,
Commander-in-Chief of the British Army, supported those who thought
a more senior officer must be found. One indeed was already in the
Peninsula. Sir Hew Dalrymple, an old Guards officer of self-evident
seniority, was already in Gibraltar as Governor and had first hand
experience of the Spanish insurrection. He was an obvious choice, and
the Horse Guards decided to appoint him to the command of the
expeditionary force. As second-in-command they appointed another
veteran Guards officer, Sir Harry Burrard.

The appointment of these two senior generals was not, however, so
much to prevent the young and vaguely suspect Sir Arthur Wellesley
being given the credit for winning what might prove to be an important
battle, as to prevent the command passing into the hands of a man the
Government had good cause both to dislike and to fear.

Sir John Moore having finally and bitterly quarrelled with the King of
Sweden had brought his army home. It was now ready to sail for the
Peninsula. If Sir John went with it, there could have been no reason, but
for the appointment of Burrard and Dalrymple, why he should not take
over from Wellesley. Several influential members of the Duke of
Portland's Ministry were anxious to avoid this at all costs.

Sir John was not a tactful man. He had disagreed with the Ministry in
the past and had not hesitated to say so. He had, to Canning's annoyance,
criticised the Foreign Office in particular. His views had a Whiggish taint;
his somewhat haughty manner and well-expressed sound sense, an air of
condemnation; his noble good looks and purity of thought and action,
an odour of disturbing sanctity. It was hoped that, if Lord Castlereagh
casually mentioned to him that his services would be welcome in Spain
as a subordinate to two officers whose names were almost unknown, he
would feel compelled to withdraw from the expedition. He did not do
so. He was angry but he would not be deflected from his duty. Instead
of two superiors, Wellesley was thus saddled with three.

He was already on the march, however, and perhaps he might yet reach
the French and prove he was not merely a sepoy general, before any of
these generals reached him.

On August 15th his eager skirmishers came up against the French near
Obidos and charged forward with such impulsive excitement that many
of them were killed. Two days later, when the French had fallen back to
their defensive line at Roliça, the same impulsiveness and reckless bravery
cost him nearly 500 men, most of whom might have been saved. But the

defensive line was broken and the army moved on to Vimiero. In the sandy estuary of the river Maceira, two miles west of the village, two further brigades landed during August 19th and 20th; and on the evening of the second day Sir Harry Burrard arrived in the sloop *Brazen*.

Wellesley went aboard to tell him that he wanted to advance; but Sir Harry did not think he should. Better to wait, he said, until Moore arrived with his 12,000 additional men. He did not go ashore as he had letters to write. 'I only wish Sir Harry had landed', Wellesley wrote gloomily to Castlereagh, 'and seen things with his own eyes.'

His gloom, however, was soon dispelled. The French moved forward that night and the next day in their white summer uniforms they advanced in columns up the hill towards them. 'I received them in line', he said years later, recalling with evident satisfaction that they came on that day towards his lines, 'with more confidence' than they ever did afterwards. And on those lines the French columns broke. As his men chased the French troops down the slopes and Wellesley saw that his victory was complete, he turned in his saddle to Sir Harry who had sensibly left the direction of the battle to the younger general's more adept eye. 'Sir Harry,' Wellesley said to him, 'now is your time to advance. The enemy are completely beaten and we shall be in Lisbon in three days.'

Sir Harry did not agree. His cautious temperament, made more cautious still by the uniformly unsuccessful expeditions in which he had been previously engaged, exerted itself once more. He ordered the pursuit to be called off. The following day 'Dowager' Dalrymple, as Wellesley was later disdainfully to call him in a letter to the Duke of Richmond, came from Gibraltar to approve of the action that 'Betty' Burrard had taken.

Sir Arthur's position, as he told Lord Castlereagh, was now a 'very delicate one'. He had never met Dalrymple before and 'it is not a very easy task to advise any man on the first day one meets him'. It was especially true of this particular man who showed himself not merely unwilling to listen to advice but resentful of its even being offered. By the time General Kellerman came towards the British lines on August 22nd, escorted by two squadrons of dragoons carrying white flags, Sir Arthur had learned his lesson. He spoke little during the six hours the generals sat discussing the terms of surrender. He did not approve of the truce and, when asked by Dalrymple to sign it, he did so reluctantly with the comment that it was an extraordinary paper.

It was indeed extraordinary, but the opportunity of following up the success of the battle had already gone and it at least provided for the evacuation of the French army from Portugal. The French, however, were to be taken home in British ships with all their stores and all that they had acquired in Portugal. When the terms of the armistice were made known in England and Portugal, the people of both countries were furious with resentment. The excitement and pleasure that the news of the great victory at Vimiero had aroused were swept away in a rush of disillusionment and anger when the text of the Convention was published.

'I don't know', Sir Arthur told his brother the day he arrived home, 'whether I am to be hanged, drawn & quartered; or roasted alive.' For not even he had escaped the abuse which was thrown indiscriminately at the names of the three generals whose signatures had endorsed the shameful armistice. They were shown in cartoons dangling grotesquely from gallows with white feathers in their hats. They were shown together as inmates of Bedlam drinking toasts over the prostrate body of a dishonoured Britannia. Comments on the Convention of Cintra, as it came to be called, were printed in the newspapers with thick black funeral borders. Indignant people told each other that Canning had summed it up nicely when he said that he should in future spell 'humiliation' with a 'Hew'.

The only senior officer spared the insults of a mercilessly vindictive country was Sir John Moore. While the Corporation of London petitioned for an enquiry into the Convention, and the pressure of public opinion forced the Government to recall Dalrymple, who with his two colleagues was to face a Board of General Officers in the Great Hall of Chelsea Hospital, Sir John remained behind in Lisbon.

A few years before he had been recognised as the Army's 'prodigy', its greatest training officer since Wolfe, its most likely aspirant to a quality of leadership which had not been seen since the death of Marlborough. Now his promise seemed never likely to be fulfilled. He was still only forty-six ard a dedicated soldier, but his friends had almost given up hope of seeing him given the opportunities of a great command. The son of a Glasgow doctor, he had obtained his ensigncy in the 51st Foot in 1776, and had served at first in Minorca and then in America in a new Regiment raised by the Duke of Hamilton; but at the peace of 1783 Hamilton's regiment was disbanded, and Moore went back to Scotland. The following year, at the age of twenty-three, he entered Parliament in the Hamilton interest and, although he never spoke, he took his duties with that conscientious care and seriousness which were already features of a remarkable temperament.

His qualities were recognised by two people who were later to be of great help to him – Pitt and the Commander-in-Chief of the Army, the Duke of York. Through their influence his rise in the army was fast. After service in the Mediterranean, in Corsica, in the West Indies, in Ireland and in Holland he was appointed to command the reserve in the Egyptian expedition. At the battle of Alexandria he was wounded for the fifth time and returned home with his reputation assured. It was 1803 and England was preparing to resist an invasion from a French army led by 'that vile, proud, ambitious, hated villain' Napoleon. At Shorncliffe on the coast of Kent a camp was being prepared for specially picked troops, who were to bear the first shock of the attack and contain it while the main force was concentrated behind them. To this camp Major-General Moore was sent. The men under his command there were soon to become the finest light infantry in Europe.

The country had need of them. There were only just over 100,000 Regulars in the Army. Two Militia bills passed in 1803 provided for the drafting of Militiamen into the Army and for the increase in strength of the Militia itself by the provision of four weeks' annual training for 200,000 men. But these numbers were paltry in comparison with the hundreds of thousands of men who had been conscripted into the armies of Napoleon. Moore was accordingly determined to make the relatively few soldiers entrusted to his care into units so highly trained, so finely disciplined, so mobile and so adaptable that they could face with confidence the more massive formations of their enemies.

France's Revolutionary armies had swept across the plains of Central Europe behind a screen of *voltigeurs* and *tirailleurs*, both protective and destructive. Their new formations had proved too formidable for the dense and compact ranks of heavy infantry that opposed them, firing muskets with the precision of the drill square. Fifty years before in America Colonel Bosquet, the brilliant Swiss officer who commanded the 60th Regiment, and Lord Howe of the 55th had taught their men to fight the French as the American rangers did, not as unthinking parts of a clumsy whole but as intelligent men with individual duties to perform in a scheme of warfare that had no set rules. It was the only way to fight in the forests of America and the West Indies, and now in Europe too the construction and training of armies was changing. It was fortunate for England that she had as Commander-in-Chief of her Army a man who, before the eighteenth century was over, recognised the necessity for training regiments that could meet the French *tirailleurs* on equal terms. The Duke of York had little talent as a fighting general but as an administrator at the Horse Guards he carried through reforms which were to alter the army for ever. In 1799 he instructed various regiments to send officers and men for a course of instruction in light infantry tactics at the newly-created camp of the Experimental Rifle Corps at Horsham. Two years later the 95th Regiment was formed and the green jackets, which the men wore so proudly, gave a name to their own regiment and to others that were to become as fine as any that the world had seen or knows. Towards the end of 1802 the 95th joined the 52nd and the 43rd

Regiments at Shorncliffe camp. Within three years Moore had made these regiments the *élite* of the army.

Every man was taught to think and to act for himself, to consider himself a craftsman with a craftsman's self-respect and pride. He was made to understand the need for his drill and exercises, and not merely to perform them. He was made healthy and he was made strong. He was persuaded to go swimming and dancing rather than drinking and whoring. He was told that it was more important to be clean and smart than to give the impression of elegance by the application of pipe clay and polish over dirt and rust. He was taught to move quickly and to think quickly, how to care for his rifle and how to fire it to the best effect, how to make use of ground in combining fire and movement. He was encouraged by example and not dragooned by fear. 'The cat-o'-nine tails is never used', an officer reported on the 52nd, 'and yet discipline is there seen in the highest state of perfection.' He was encouraged by a spirit of competition, by the award of badges and cockades for marksmanship and good behaviour. He was encouraged above all by the passionate enthusiasm of Moore himself.

Tall and extremely good-looking, strong and upright, the very look of the general inspired confidence and a wish to please. He was known to be heroically brave, wholly uncorrupted and incorruptible. His words of praise or smiles of friendship were like benedictions; his scorn and contempt for those who had not lived up to his high standards were merciless and shaming. There was something god-like about him. There was also, his enemies said with more than a little truth behind the malice, something of the prig. Such uncompromising virtue, such conscious rectitude; so thorough a familiarity with the esoteric military writings of Tielke, Sontag and de Rottenburg; so completely sinless a life, were not easily forgiven in a man who spurned the uses of tact and affability. He had in addition the displeasing capacity for being almost never wrong. He had above all the tiresome ability to arouse in his admirers that kind of veneration which implies disapprobation of those less perfect.

Senior officers, for instance, who sat down to dinner at Walmer Castle with Mr. Pitt were made sometimes to feel conscious of an underlying rebuke when their host read out to them letters written to him by his favourite general whom he had caused to be made a Knight of the Bath. He read them out with many comments as to their grace of style and sensibility, with a wish that other generals wrote as well. His niece, Lady Hester Stanhope, could not but agree with him. Whomsoever he admired, she too would admire. Her brother Charles, an officer in the 50th Regiment, encouraged her admiration which in time became passionate. She would have no one speak against Sir John. An old general once presumed in her presence to make some mildly critical comment about him at which she turned furiously on him and told him that he was nothing but a 'paralytic old Kangaroo'.

Moore, for his part, found Lady Hester entrancing. He often came to visit her at Walmer and, after her uncle's death, to her London house in Montagu Square. He had never been in love, except perhaps with the seventeen-year-old Caroline Fox, daughter of General H. E. Fox, under whom he had served in the Mediterranean. Miss Fox was, he once told his friend Colonel Anderson, the only woman he had ever considered marrying, but she was after all only a child and he never offered her marriage, characteristically maintaining that he was unwilling to 'influence her to an irretrievable error for her own future contentment'. Lady Hester, however, was nearly thirty and a woman of an incomparably greater independence of mind. She spoke brilliantly with a delicious combination of wit and superficial malice. She was at once flippant and serious, irreverent and sympathetic. She had a face too angularly masculine for beauty, but she was so wonderfully alive that her features seemed to disappear in a kind of bewildering radiance. Like most domineering women she longed for domination and for love. She was sensual and Moore excited her. Once she asked her brother if he agreed that his general was physically the perfect example of a man. Yes, Charles said, and with sudden enthusiasm and unconscious cruelty added, 'But Hester, you should see him in his bath. He is like a god!'

It was a dispiriting phrase. For he *was* like a god, and had offered her only friendship. When he had gone to Portugal she imagined that he had intended much more than friendship and that one day they would be married. It was an illusion she never lost.

Left behind in Montagu Square, she championed her hero's cause with determined energy. Now that he was by common consent the only able senior officer still with the army in the Peninsula, there was, she insisted, no reason why he should not be appointed to command it. The King agreed with her. But there was still opposition in the Cabinet. Lord Castlereagh was lukewarm, George Canning was openly against the appointment, and, although he had been her uncle's friend and she had herself once loved him, she never asked the Foreign Secretary to Montagu Square again.

Despite Canning's objections, however, the tide of opinion in favour of Moore was irresistible. On 25th September, 1808, Lord Castlereagh wrote him a letter from Downing Street:

His Majesty, having determined to employ a corps of his troops, of not less than 30,000 infantry and 5,000 cavalry, in the North of Spain, to co-operate with the Spanish armies in the expulsion of the French from that Kingdom, has been graciously pleased to entrust to you the Command in Chief of this force.

Leaving a garrison in Portugal he was to advance into Spain with 20,000 men. Between 15,000 and 17,000 more were being sent out to Corunna under Lieutenant-General Sir David Baird. When they joined him he would have a greater force than any that had been collected since the war began.

2

Moore in Command

'The army, which has been appropriated by His Majesty to the defence of Spain and Portugal, is not merely a considerable part of the dispensable force of this country. It is, in fact, the British army.'

George Canning

THE CHANCE that Moore had always longed for had come at last. 'There has been no such command since Marlborough', he wrote in his diary. 'How they came to pitch upon me I cannot say, for they have given sufficient proof of not being partial to me.'

The responsibilities of this command, he realised at once, were enormous. 'The army, which has been appropriated by His Majesty to the defence of Spain and Portugal,' the Foreign Secretary told his friend Hookham Frere, expressing an important truth which was never to leave Moore's mind, 'is not merely a considerable part of the dispensable force of this country. It is, in fact, the British army. . . . Another army it has not to send.'

The army might be reinforced, but it could not be replaced. With its intended strength of 35,000 men it could not hope to meet the French on anything like equal terms, and, envisaging the possible defeat of the hastily formed Spanish armies before the British could arrive to back them up, the Duke of York, with his usual sound sense, drew up for the information of the Government a formal minute in which he suggested that the army should be increased to a strength of not less than 60,000 men. He showed in detail how these men could be provided without detriment to any of the country's other commitments.

The Government, however, were in an optimistic mood. Their military agents in Spain sent home encouraging reports of the measures being taken by the people to turn out the French aggressors. Much indeed had already been achieved. General Castaños with a ragged but fiercely determined Andalusian army had forced General Dupont to surrender at Bailen, south of the Sierra Morena; Joseph had withdrawn in alarm as far as Vitoria, beyond the Ebro river in Navarra, and Castaños had reoccupied Madrid in triumph; General Palafox directing the defence of Saragossa had been helped by all its citizens, one of whom, a young woman who continued firing a gun while her brother and lover lay dead at her feet, was to live in men's memories for ever. By heroism such as this the French had been pushed back with heavy losses towards the Pyrenees.

The early success, the bravery and the enthusiasm, however, gave only the illusion of strength. The victories had been won by sudden, unrelated upsurges of courage and determination in isolated provinces. To the Andalusian, the victory at Bailen was a triumph for Andalusia, not for Spain; the defence of Saragossa was the pride of Aragon; the forced retreat of the French across the Somosierra Pass, the pride of Castile. It was grudgingly accepted that the French could not be pushed completely out of Spain without a combined effort by the armies – sometimes no more than untrained bands of armed students and peasants – of each province. But how this could be brought about no one could say. Each provincial Junta refused to consider allowing its army to be commanded by a general from another province; each Junta competed with its neighbour to obtain the largest share of the arms and ammunition which the British Government had instructed its harassed military agents to distribute; no Junta considered the Supreme Junta, which was eventually set up in response to repeated British suggestions, of greater importance than itself.

The jealousies engendered by this passionate provincialism were so acute that it seemed for a time the country would slip into civil war. The Junta of Galicia refused to co-operate with the Castilian Juntas unless a formal treaty of alliance were signed and ratified. The Asturian Juntas refused to supply the Galician army under General Joachim Blake when it passed through their province, although the stores it needed had been sent out from England and lay unused in the Asturian port of Gijon. Here also money sent out for the help of the Junta of Leon was detained and appropriated by the Asturians. The members of the Junta of Seville pocketed the pay of their troops, and yet threatened to send their unpaid army to attack Granada whose Junta refused to recognise their supremacy.

The local gentry and clergy and the lesser nobles who, by the collapse of the central Government and the organisation of these provincial Juntas, had their first taste of real power and influence were utterly incapable either of exercising authority or of thinking of the struggle as a national one. The grandees and the nobles of Madrid were as incompetent, as selfish and as corrupt, without having even the saving grace of provincial pride. Most of them had fled from danger; some had collaborated with the French and had now gone to Paris; many of those that remained contributed to the defence of their country gifts which would have been unworthy of their farriers.

Despite the state of the country and the quarrels of its self-appointed leaders, the wild optimism that had followed the victory at Bailen persisted. In a despatch written at the time that Moore received his instructions, Major-General Lord William Bentinck, who had been sent to Madrid as a British representative pending an appointment by the Foreign Office, gave his opinion that this optimism was not merely unjustified but dangerous. 'I am at every moment more and more convinced', he wrote, 'that a blind confidence in their own strength, and natural slowness, are the rocks upon which this good ship runs the risk of being wrecked.'

Moore had a similarly melancholy foreboding. But for the moment there were other problems which more immediately concerned him.

He had only a few weeks left to get his army out of Portugal before the autumn rains came on. Although Dalrymple had been authorised by the Government to cross the frontier into Spain as soon as the news of Vimiero was received in London, little had been done in preparation for the move. For more than four weeks the army had been waiting in the dusty heat of the late summer while Junot's army unhurriedly departed. Two brigades under Lieutenant-General the Hon. John Hope had been sent to the frontier at Elvas to persuade the Spanish general Galuzzo, who refused to recognise the terms of the Convention of Cintra, to abandon his siege of the French garrison at Elvas. But the rest of the army remained in idleness near Lisbon, growing impatient and irritable, lax and unhealthy. In the large camp at Queluz, where the air was heavy with dust and flies, one of the officers whose tent was pitched there said that:

> What with the great heat, the cold nights, the eating of fruit and the drinking of young wine, the health of the army became so much impaired that typhus and dysentery broke out and spread rapidly, affecting even the inhabitants of villages lying close to the camp. The pestilential stench of our slaughter-house refuse, also contributed somewhat to the trouble; while, in addition, a huge hospital was installed in one of the wings of the castle, not far behind and below our stores depot, and separated from it only by a long ditch which was used as a latrine by the dysentery patients, and was not 500 yards away. Infection was bound to occur.

Much of the illness was brought on by excessive drinking; and on October 9th, when orders were issued to the various regiments to hold themselves in readiness for an advance towards Spain, the troops were at the same time warned by their new commander of the dangers of such heavy drinking:

The Lieutenant-General sees with much concern the great number of [sick] and that it daily increases. The General assures the troops that it is owing to their own intemperance that so many of them are rendered incapable of marching against the Enemy; and having stated this, he feels confident that he need say no more to British soldiers to ensure their sobriety.

Certainly the prospect of advancing into Spain 'brightened the spirits of the army', and cases of drunkenness decreased. The possibility of advancing, however, with anything but the army's barest requirements was remote. In the weeks that the army had been waiting at Queluz, it had been found impossible to collect sufficient transport to move it. Dalrymple had been sent out with a totally inadequate military train and the wagons that had since been collected were both too cumbersome and too few. The country carts were peculiarly primitive. The axles which turned with the solid wheels were attached by leather straps to a wooden yoke behind the bullocks' horns, and, although the bullocks were 'shod with a kind of iron shoe, and in this way', so a commissary reported, seemed able to 'drag a load of about half a ton up hill and down dale, along the roughest mountain roads with the greatest ease', they would not move with such facility when the autumn rains reduced the mountain roads to muddy tracks. All the hackney carriages in Lisbon had been requisitioned and their superstructures removed on orders of the Portuguese Government; but these too were to slip and slither in the mud of the mountain passes.

The distribution of supplies was, for Moore, as great a problem as their movement. The Commissariat was, in his own phrase, much wanting in experience. He did not think that in its present form it could cope with the administrative problems of supplying so large an army. Its more important posts would have to be filled by men outside the department. 'The department itself must not be looked to', he told Lord Castlereagh. 'In it, I am persuaded, proper Officers will not be found; but men of business and resource are to be found in London; and it is such men only who are fit for the higher branches of the Commissariat.'

The more junior officials, many of whom were Germans, were temporary employees and almost universally despised by the soldiers as being both dishonest and incompetent. 'From all I can observe', one of their critics said, making an observation which would have found general agreement, 'the service would be greatly benefited by the dismissal of the whole Commissariat . . . . Nothing could be more true than a brother or relation of Lord Rosslyn's saying, when being appointed commissary to an army, that he was going out to cheat the King and starve the troops.'

In some cases the contempt was justified; but in most cases junior commissaries were conscientious if unimaginative men who did their best in conditions of appalling difficulty, only to be dismissed when the war was over. They had grounds for feeling ill-used.

The officers of the Quartermaster-General's staff and, indeed, of all the staff of the army's administrative departments were similarly abused. As with the commissaries it was not so much that they were wilfully negligent as wholly inexperienced. They went forward to organise the collection of magazines and stores, to survey roads, to requisition buildings, without any clear idea of what the army would require, of how fast it could move, or of what constituted an adequate route. Hardly any of them spoke Portuguese or Spanish; none of them was supplied with adequate maps or had previously had to deal with the problems of logistics on so large and difficult a scale.

On the day that he acknowledged receipt of the Government's instructions, Moore told Castlereagh that he was at that time 'without equipment of any kind, either for the carriages of the light baggage, artillery store, commissariat store, or any other appendage of an army, and without a magazine formed on any of the routes by which we are to march'. More than a week later, he was little better placed. 'I have no hope of getting forward at present', he reported on October 18th,

with more than the light baggage of the troops, the ammunition immediately necessary for the service of the artillery, and a very scanty supply of medicines. The depot which I wish to establish at Almeida, I cannot wait for; but I hope the experience which is acquired in setting the troops in motion, will enable the Commissariat, when we are gone, to forward what is wanted for Almeida.

'The arrangement for supplies should have been made', he complained to Lord William Bentinck three days later in a letter which clearly shows his irritation,

and the information respecting roads should have been got before the march began – but when I got the command nothing of this sort had been done. They talked of going into Spain as of going into Hyde Park; nobody seemed aware of what an arduous task it was; and the season of the year admitting of no delay, there was a necessity for beginning the march, and trusting to information and supplies as we got on.

He had originally intended to advance from Lisbon to the frontier at Almeida by two parallel routes: one almost due north to Coimbra on the

Mondego river and then north-east through Celorico to Almeida; the other along the bank of the Tagus to Abrantes and then turning north through Castello Branco and Guarda. The two brigades under General Hope at Elvas would have to take a third route through Estramadura. The three routes would meet somewhere in the plains of Old Castile, and then the army could move on together from Salamanca for a concentration at Valladolid or perhaps further north still at Burgos.

These seemed perfectly feasible routes from the *Mapa Militar* and the other maps which George Murray, the Quartermaster-General, had found in Lisbon; but the maps were misleading. Portuguese engineer officers advised the British Headquarters that the two routes from Lisbon were unsuitable for cavalry and impossible for artillery. Captain Delaney of George Murray's staff and other officers who had inspected the mountain roads of the Portuguese province of Beira agreed with this opinion. It seemed, in fact, that there was no way of getting artillery from Lisbon to Almeida at this time of year. The guns themselves could be taken there, but their wheels and axles would be knocked to pieces on the journey. 'Every information agreed', Moore wrote home, 'that neither of the northern routes was fit for artillery or could be recommended for cavalry.' And he decided accordingly that he must send all but the lightest of his guns with his two cavalry regiments to the south, to join Hope's circuitous route through Estramadura.

The route which Hope was to take followed the main Madrid road as far as Talavera, where it turned north to link up with the other routes in Old Castile. Elvas is 160 miles from Salamanca as the crow flies; by this route it is more than twice as far. Although the cavalry and artillery left to join Hope's division on October 18th, it was to be several weeks before they met Moore's main force again, and by then the whole aspect of the campaign had altered. Moore knew the risk he was taking by separating his army; he knew that he might be without an adequate striking force for as long as five weeks once his horses and guns had left him. And despite assurances that he had no alternative, he confessed that he watched the cavalry go with an anxious heart, wondering if the decision was justified.

There were other problems too. Warned that he must get across the mountains before the heavy rains turned the mountain streams into impassable torrents, and aware of the importance 'of even the name of a British army in Spain', he was, he assured the Government, 'hurrying as much as possible'. But he was hampered not only by an ill-trained staff and Commissariat, but also by a crippling lack of money.

The Treasury had failed to supply him with bullion and the Portuguese contractors had a horror of Government bills and promissory notes. His military chest contained no more than £25,000. The cost of hiring transport would alone come to more than that. Eventually he found a merchant prepared to supply the army with some stores on credit. But within a few weeks the man was bankrupt and his promises were unfulfilled. 'It is impossible to describe the embarrassment we are thrown into', Moore told Castlereagh when reporting on his need for cash.

> Nothing but abundance of money, and prompt payments will compensate, when we begin to move, for the want of experience and ability of our Commissariat . . . . It is my intention to make the troops find their own meat, and to call upon the Commissary for bread and wine and forage only. This would be attended with many good effects, besides easing the Commissariat. The troops would be satisfied with less meat and gradually learn to live upon what the country produced in greatest abundance; but to adopt this plan I must be certain of money to pay them which at present I am not.

The problem of feeding the army was increased by the large numbers of women and children who had come out with it. The official number of wives permitted to each company on active service had been limited to a maximum of six, but this had been greatly exceeded. Officers had looked the other way when women in excess of the allotted number had slipped aboard the transports; and many more women had smuggled themselves out since. In an effort to get rid of them, Moore offered them their passage back to England and on October 10th a General Order was published to this effect:

> As in the course of the long march which the army is about to undertake and where no carts will be allowed, the women would unavoidably be exposed to the greatest hardship and distress, commanding officers are, therefore, desired to use their endeavours to prevent as many as possible, particularly those having young children, or such as are not stout, or equal to fatigue, from following the army. Those who remain will be left with the heavy luggage of the regiments. An officer will be charged to draw their rations, and they will be sent to England by the first good opportunity; and when landed, they will receive the same allowance which they would have been entitled to, if they had not embarked, to enable them to reach their homes.

Only a few women accepted the offer. The great majority refused to leave their men and prepared to march taking their children with them across the mountains.

The day after this Order was published the advance guard of the army left for Almeida under Brigadier-General Robert Anstruther, a forty-year-old officer who had distinguished himself in Egypt and at Vimiero. He was in good spirits, full of hope and confidence. If Napoleon 'beats us', he cheerfully wrote back to Headquarters, 'we shall be like the rest of the world. If we beat him, we shall be like ourselves alone.'

Moore's was not a temperament, however, which could accept the possibility of defeat with so engaging a detachment. He was concerned and anxious and he could not hide it. Brigadier-General Charles Stewart, the Marquess of Londonderry's son and Lord Castlereagh's half-brother, who was given command of the cavalry with Hope's division, thought the Commander of the Forces 'wanted confidence in *himself* – he was afraid of *responsibility* – he *underrated* the qualities of his own troops, and greatly *overrated* those of his adversary . . . a most excellent but over-cautious man'.

Stewart was a dashing and talented cavalry officer, but an intriguing narrow-minded man who made much of his relationship with the Secretary-for-War. He was, in Moore's opinion, 'a very silly fellow'.

There were, nevertheless, those who agreed with him. A cavalry officer said of Moore:

> Although an officer of eminent bravery and tried ability in subordinate commands, now that he was called upon to conduct a considerable force in circumstances of peculiar difficulties proved lamentably deficient in those qualities of decision and firmness which he had so often displayed on former occasions.

Another found him 'too much concerned about detail and, moreover, hypochondriacal'.

But these were minority judgments. 'Sir John Moore', Commissary August Schaumann said, 'is respected everywhere because of his high sense of honour, his jealousy of his country's fame, his great knowledge, and the warmth of his feelings. In addition he is a brave and experienced soldier, and a perfect gentleman.'

What particularly endeared him to his officers, a young Ensign of the 28th Regiment reported, was his

> constant habit of speaking to every officer of his army whom he met, whatever his rank, asking such questions as tended to elicit useful information, and in the most good-humoured and courteous manner making such remarks as indirectly called forth the most strenuous endeavours of all to a full discharge of their duties . . . . Although anxiously employed in forming magazines and depots and organising the whole material of the army, yet [he] appeared to be continually in our ranks.

Each one of Moore's divisional commanders was able to command a similar respect. The oldest of the three, Major-General Alexander Mackenzie Fraser, at fifty-two had seen even more active service than Moore himself. He was a Highlander and although a man of strong nerves and inflexible courage he treated his men with the gentleness of a devoted, if sometimes disappointed, father. He was a competent general but not an outstanding one.

The Hon. John Hope, however, in Wellington's later opinion, was 'the ablest man in the Peninsular War'. Like Fraser he was a personal friend of Moore and had also been with him in Sweden. A son of the Earl of Hopetoun, he was a good-looking man with a straight back and an unmistakable air of authority about him. He was forty-three and enjoying his first important independent command with the essential duty of bringing up the heavy guns and the cavalry into Spain from Elvas.

General the Hon. Edward Paget, a son of the Earl of Uxbridge, who was sent to join him at Elvas and then to take an infantry division through Alcantara and Coria to Ciudad Rodrigo, was another man of exceptional talents. He was the younger brother of Lord Paget, the general commanding the cavalry under Sir David Baird, soon to land at Corunna. Of both these remarkable brothers much was later to be heard.

The fourth division, which was due to follow Fraser from Lisbon, was temporarily commanded by Major-General William Carr Beresford. Alone of Moore's chosen commanders he was an ugly man. His left eye, injured many years before in a shooting accident, was discoloured and static. It gave to the rugged features of his weather-beaten face an appearance that his soldiers found disconcerting even when he was not angry, which he frequently was. The illegitimate son of an Irish peer, he had been to a military school at Strasbourg and had been intermittently on active service since the age of seventeen. He was now forty, and was believed to have a more powerful body than any man in the army.

Although these generals and their brigadiers, in accordance with the customs of their time, appointed officers to their staffs with more regard to their birth and influence than to their competence, Moore's own staff officers were men of undoubted gifts. George Murray, the Quartermaster-General and Henry Clinton, the Adjutant-General, were both men whom Moore knew well and implicitly trusted. His Military Secretary, John Colborne, was only twenty-one, and already a man of exceptional talent. He had entered the 20th Regiment from Christ's Hospital at the age of sixteen and later became a field-marshal without ever having purchased a step in his promotion. Tall and athletic and with those noble good looks that resembled his master's, he was Moore's devoted admirer and remained so for the remaining fifty-five years of his distinguished life.

A few nights before he left Lisbon for the Spanish frontier, he accompanied his General to a dreary farewell banquet given by a rich and distinguished member of the Portuguese Government. Usually after the meal on such occasions the guests would play cards. It was known, however, that Sir John did not play and his host devised a different sort of entertainment. Portraits of his ancestors were paraded through the dining-room by servants while he gave a lecture on their interests and achievements. The last portrait was of an officer who had served under Lord Galway a hundred years before. The manner of his sad death was not mentioned, but Moore knew what it was.

He said softly to Colborne, with a kind of prophetic apprehension, 'He was killed in Spain.'

PART TWO

The Advance

3

Lisbon to Salamanca

'I hope I am not a prophet, but if the English troops don't save Spain, I think the Spaniards can't.'

Major Charles Napier, 50th Regiment

ON OCTOBER 11TH the leading regiments filed out of the camp at Queluz and moved to the east along the banks of the Tagus in the faint autumn sunshine. On the General's orders the men were wearing in their hats as a compliment to the Spanish nation 'red cockades with the words *Viva Ferdinando Settimo*' stamped on them in gold. They marched in the fields beside the wide river with their drums tapping in the warm air, soft ground underfoot and partridges and quail flying across the sky above the olive trees. The valley was full of wild flowers and lovely brambles and aromatic shrubs – thyme, myrtle, sage and lavender, woodbine, rosemary, strawberry and rock-rose. Men stepped surreptitiously from the ranks to pick bunches of buttercups and poppies and threw them to the girls in the narrow white streets of the villages. At Abrantes they crossed the Tagus by ferry, between the ships up from Lisbon with their cargoes of food and ammunition, and then marched on towards the frontier, through pine woods and vineyards and cork forests and across granite-studded heaths, past convents and Moorish castles and churches crumbling with age.

The further inland they marched the more desolate the countryside became. The pleasant little towns of the valley gave place to gloomy hill villages where tall, silent houses with black grilles at the windows and peeling plaster on the walls leant towards each other across the narrow cobbled streets; where peasants in dun-coloured cloaks, smocks of straw and wooden clogs surveyed the passing red-coats with suspicious eyes; and there was a smell in the air, constant and pervading, of sour wine, cooking oil and open drains. The men spent their nights in the long, cold corridors of tiled convents and in the lofty, acrid-smelling stables of half-ruined castles; while the officers found private billets with priests and officials, and eventually became used to sleeping in beds made up on the floor and undressing under the close and silently curious surveillance of

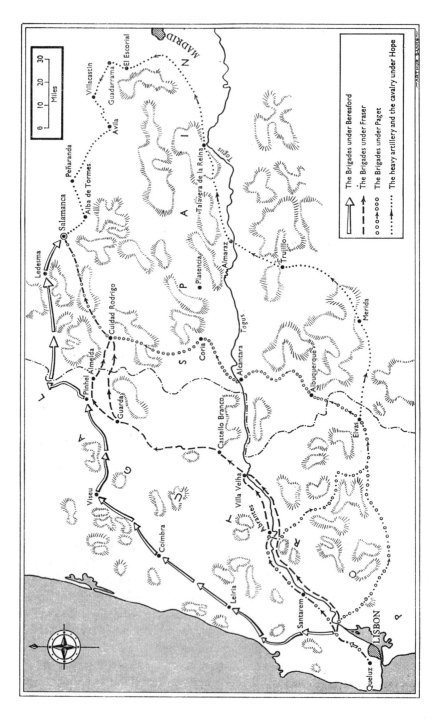

The advance of the British Forces from Lisbon to Salamanca

entire families. They were offered food with a kind of servile reluctance which irritated them all, and when it came it usually revolted them. The principal dish consisted of a strong meat, oily and evil-smelling, into which were thrown quantities of chopped vegetables, herbs, bread, beans and garlic. The wine was sour and the water undrinkable. When asked for something that he had not got, the host would reply by pressing his tobacco-stained finger-nails behind his teeth and letting them spring forward in a rush of garlic-flavoured breath. The British officers did not like the Portuguese and as the route led higher up into the mountains they liked them less.

The weather too, adding to their growing dissatisfaction, began to break and the air became oppressive with the threat of rain. At Villa Velha, once a large town but now consisting only of a few mean-looking houses lying under the brow of an overhanging hill, the rain began to drizzle down in a continuous, dampening shower. By the beginning of November, when the troops had begun their long ascent into the mountains beyond Castello Branco, the clouds finally burst and the rain poured blindingly down.

The mountain tracks became quagmires and in places the rain rushed down from the heights in torrents, overflowing into the ravines and forcing the men to shelter behind protective clefts in the dark rock wall. Weak, exhausted bullocks and mules, pulling at ammunition carts and wagon-loads of biscuit, would stumble on the steep, water-rutted tracks, and hired muleteers or soldiers would run forward and try to push and tug the wagon up the pass. Often they could not stop it slipping backwards and the whole load, beast and burden, ran backwards down the slope, scraping, rumbling, splashing, bellowing, to plunge into the abyss. And often the Portuguese guides lost their way in the mist and the leading regiments found themselves astray among impassable mountain paths and goat-tracks. Throwing rocks down into the misty air, beyond the edges of the track, the soldiers listened for the echoing crash as the rocks hit the bottom of the ravine, and sometimes listened in vain as they fell down through the immeasurable depths.

The days were short and the long nights when the rain had stopped were bitterly cold. The icy wind howled in the mountain passes as the men lay down to sleep. One night, a soldier of the 71st remembered, was 'one of the severest nights of cold' he had ever endured in his life. 'At that time', he wrote afterwards, 'we wore long hair, formed into a club at the back of our heads. Mine was frozen to the ground in the morning; and when I attempted to rise, my limbs refused to support me for some time. I felt the most excruciating pains all over my body, before the blood began to circulate.'

These nights of biting cold and days of blinding rain continued as the army edged slowly forward into Spain. And it was not until the first week of November that Anstruther's leading brigade reached the frontier fortress of Almeida. Moore arrived there on November 8th. He had come on the Guarda road from Villa Velha and had not found it too difficult. He felt sure that he had been ill-advised to send his heavy artillery by the circuitous route through Estramadura and New Castile and wrote to tell Hope so. If anything adverse happened, he told him, he would not be able to plead that he had split his army through necessity. 'The road we are now travelling', he wrote, 'is practicable for artillery. The brigade under Wilmot has already reached Guarda and as far as I have already seen the road presents few obstacles and those easily surmounted.' Five days later, however, he realised that the Portuguese engineers had no doubt been right. The leading regiments were finding the going hard enough, the ones that had followed and the light artillery were finding it appalling. Days of rain and the passage of thousands of troops and carts had reduced the surface of the tracks to a succession of ruts and potholes and loose stones. On the 13th Moore saw the 6-pounders on their creaking, battered carriages and wrote again to Hope to assure him that he was moving by the only practicable road for heavy artillery. A week later he told Castlereagh that the light artillery had got through with 'infinite difficulty' and that the roads were the worst he ever saw.

The army had crossed now into Spain. The frontier was marked by a little rivulet, so small that, when they were told they were entering Spain, the soldiers stopped to straddle it, one foot in each country, looking at each other and laughing. Suddenly their spirits had risen. They marched down on to the Salamanca plain, singing cheerfully. A new country was open before then. It was strikingly unlike the one they had left. 'No change, whether in the face of the country, in men and manners, can be greater than that immediately perceptible upon entering Spain from Portugal', Sir John Moore noted in his diary. 'The advantage is entirely on the side of the Spaniards.' Not everyone agreed with him. A German officer took quite an opposite view of the contrast. 'What a difference', he wrote, 'between the friendly, hospitable Portuguese and these disobliging Spaniards! Everyone here is grave, monosyllabic and gloomy.'

The soldiers too did not care for the Spaniards. Their houses were cleaner, their farms well stocked, the fields well cultivated; but their pride was mistaken for indifference, their natural wariness for suspicion and conceit. They seemed to resent the foreigners as they might have resented an army of occupation. Standing in the streets in their long, tight, laced and buttoned pantaloons with red sashes at the waist, their split-sleeved waistcoats and brown mantles they gazed at the passing ranks with an indolent and haughty indifference which was at once disturbing and irritating. Smoking cigarettes, which they passed silently from hand to hand, they watched the marching ranks impassively, their dark eyes shadowed beneath the enormous brims of low-crowned hats. Only at the sight of the women and children, following the army with the baggage carts, did they seem to evince a momentary interest. The nuns with whom these women were occasionally housed for the night, however, displayed an interest which was close to fascination. They crowded round them, all talking excitedly at the same time; and on one occasion they went so far as to undress one of them 'to examine her person'.

When the army halted for the night the soldiers tried to make friends but could not. They found that the Spaniards, 'more than ordinarily self-important in consequence of their late achievements, were quick to take offence, even where none was intended, and not indisposed to provoke and engage in broils'. The officers fared little better than they had done in Portugal and sometimes not as well. As guests in private houses they found themselves, as often as not, completely excluded from the life of the family, and left to eat their meals alone. They were given the impression that the services of their army were not only unnecessary but unwanted.

'I hope I am not a prophet,' an officer of the 50th told his mother,

> but if the British troops don't save Spain, I think the Spaniards can't, for so vain are they that already they talk of invading France, forgetting that the best general and 300,000 of the second best troops in the world are to be conquered first. They all seem to be well inclined to throw off the yoke of the priesthood; and as they are up to any class of villainy I should not be surprised if they murdered the monks and destroyed the convents. By the bye, the aforesaid monks are the fattest people in Spain, and there are 200,000 of them, and their bishops very impudent, refusing to allow British officers into their houses although they were regularly *billeted*, for which the Spanish officers who accompanied us called them damn cooks and *wig-makers* to their faces.

The British officers had an even lower opinion of the priesthood. Commissary Schaumann said that when the Spanish people, on whom he had been billeted, heard that he was a German from Hanover they asked him 'where that country was, and whether it had any towns, and was inhabited by Christians'. The priest, who in Spain was 'always an oracle', replied for him 'with much affected importance':

> Hanover is a country that lies between Denmark and Sweden. Like those two countries it is inhabited chiefly by heathens and heretics who worship

Luther; that is why God has given them long winters and barren soil – a miserable land! For it has neither wine, oil, chestnuts, nor melons. The inhabitants do a little cattle-rearing and agriculture, but they are half wild.

Another officer had a similar experience. He produced a map of Spain to a group of friars:

It cost me at least a quarter of an hour's labour to make them comprehend the relative position of the principal Spanish towns. But it was quite beyond my power to make them understand the situation of the British Isles, which they were very anxious to ascertain; or to persuade them that our country is separated both from France and Spain by the ocean.

The ignorance and gullibility of the Spaniards occasionally led to serious misunderstandings. On their march from Elvas one of the brigades of General Hope's division spent the night in the village of Fraxiollo, where the peasants were intrigued by the uniform of the 92nd Regiment. 'Being the only regiment here at this time that wore the Highland garb,' Sergeant Roberts of the 92nd indignantly wrote,

the people were struck with the novelty of the dress and wished to know to what country its wearers belonged. The 71st from having been in South America possessed a smattering of the Spanish language and they told the credulous natives that the 92nd were a set of cowards and transported felons who were doomed to wear that costume as a badge of disgrace. The Spaniards were quite indignant at the British Government for sending such a set of ladroons into their country. Indeed, so far did the matter go, that the mayor of the town actually refused to supply us with rations.

The clergy, while not, of course, sharing the ignorance of their flocks, seemed to have shared their confidence in the invincibility of Spanish arms and to have added to this confidence an undisguised contempt for the British and a predilection for the French. 'The English will advance', the treasurer to the Bishop of Ciudad Rodrigo said in the presence of an English officer, 'now that there are no Frenchmen in the way.'

The confident hope that the Spanish armies could alone keep the French out of the way was, however, soon to be broken. On November 13th Moore entered Salamanca and realised for the first time the full absurdity of Spanish pretensions. On his arrival in the town he was greeted with exquisite courtesy by the young President of the Junta, the Marqués de Cerralbo, who told him that his house and servants were entirely at his disposal. The Marqués's major-domo had instructions to ensure that the English General and his staff were given everything that they required.

'Impossible!' said Moore. 'I am going to have people with me every day. I cannot think of putting you to so much expense.'

'Well,' the Marqués replied, 'if you will not let me give you everything, you shall not stay in my house.'

Moore gave way, bowed his head graciously in agreement and followed the Marqués through the narrow cobbled streets, past extravagant fifteenth-century buildings fading into decay, high walls of yellow and orange-coloured stone, and studded doors with grilled judases, to the impressively arched and pillared Palacio de San Boal. When the two men were alone the Marqués told Moore that he had some rather unfortunate news to tell him. The Army of Estramadura, commanded by the twenty-year-old Conde de Belveder, had retired from Burgos and the French were in possession of the town.

A few hours later he was woken by an officer who brought him news of other reverses. An express message from General Pignatelli, the Governor of the province, had been handed in at Headquarters. The Governor was sorry to have to inform Sir John Moore that General Joachim Blake had suffered a slight reverse. The following day he was told that Blake had suffered two further reverses at Espinosa.

Despite the calm, off-hand, almost confident tone of the messages, the Spanish defeats were disastrous. After weeks of quarrelling with his rivals, General Blake had decided to act alone. On October 31st he led the Army of Galicia against Ney at Durango where his ill-fed, wretchedly clothed and inadequately armed troops were turned back in confusion to Bilbao. By November 7th Napoleon himself was at Vitoria with three widely separated Spanish armies at his mercy. He struck quickly. On November 10th Blake was crushed near Espinosa and on the following day sent hurtling back across the Cantabrian mountains. The Conde de Belveder's Army of Estramadura was all but destroyed at the village of Gamonal, north of Burgos; and Burgos itself, the base of that army at the beginning of Napoleon's advance, was now the advanced base of an almost unscathed French army rushing on to Valladolid. Within a week Napoleon had thrown his magnificent troops through the centre of the Spanish defences and had taken possession of Valladolid which only a few days before had been suggested to Moore as a suitable rendezvous for the junction of the British forces.

That this junction could ever now be effected seemed unlikely. But, without any exact information as to their movements from his Spanish allies, Moore remained for the moment in ignorance of the real danger of his position. That the danger existed, however, he could not doubt.

On November 15th, in his bare room at the Palacio de San Boal in Salamanca, he wrote briefly in his diary:

> The positions of the Spanish armies, I have never been able to understand. They are separated, the one in Biscay, the other in Aragon, on the two flanks of the French, leaving the whole country of Spain exposed to their incursion, and leaving the British army exposed to be attacked before it is united.

Even if the French did not continue their advance, it would be many days yet before his own army could unite. For only that very day, nearly three hundred miles to the north-west, had a troop of the 7th Hussars led Sir David Baird's cavalry out of Corunna on the long road to Salamanca.

4

Salamanca

'We have no business here, but being here it would never do to abandon the Spaniards without a struggle.'

Sir John Moore

FOR ALMOST A FORTNIGHT since the morning of October 13th, Sir David Baird had waited with furious impatience in Corunna harbour for permission from the local Junta of Galicia to bring his troops ashore.

There were insufficient supplies in the area for so large an army, he was assured. The Spaniards' own Galician army, under General Blake, had already taken everything. Would he consider landing at Santander or even Gijon? Sir David would consider no such thing. Well then, the Junta's spokesman said, the Supreme Junta would have to be consulted. If Sir David would be good enough to wait until directions were received from Aranjuez, there would be no objection to the officers coming ashore to visit the town in the meantime.

Sir David had never been an even-tempered man. As a young captain in the 73rd Highlanders he had been wounded and taken prisoner in India and with the bullet still in his wound he had been chained to a fellow prisoner. When the news reached his mother in Scotland that her son was treated in this way, she acknowledged the fact of his savage temper in an observation of maternal percipience. 'God help', she said, 'the puir child chained to our Davie.'

Twenty years had passed since his release and he was now over fifty. Age had not mellowed him. 'He is a bloody old bad-tempered Scotchman', one of his officers thought. But although it was true that he had, as Wellington himself was later to observe, a sulky, touchy, jealous disposition with no talent and no tact, he was 'a gallant, hard-headed, lion-hearted officer'. He passed the time of his enforced inactivity by despatching a series of full-blooded complaints to Moore and to everyone else he could think of; while his officers, accepting the Spanish decision with a more philosophical resignation, went into Corunna to enjoy themselves.

There was, however, little opportunity for enjoyment. 'With the exception of a few of the principal streets,' a chaplain thought, 'nothing can surpass their abominable filth, nor could I describe it minutely, without exhibiting the most disgusting pictures.' Even the principal streets were unpleasant to walk in, for although clean and well-paved a gloomy atmosphere hung about them. They were swept each day by a gang of chained convicts the sound of whose 'iron fetters clanking upon the ear' was persistently melancholy. The architecture of the town was unimaginative and boring. The numerous *miradores* – those structures of folding glass panels which protect the balconies of Spanish houses from the Atlantic winds – emphasised the bleakness of the weather. The goods in the shops were expensive and of foreign make; the local manufactures appearing mainly to consist of 'impossible-looking hats and sour tasting chocolate'.

The hotels, Captain Gordon of the 15th Hussars reported, were

> very indifferent and the conduct of the landlords was quite unaccountable. Upon the first arrival of the British they were perfectly willing to accommodate small parties of officers with board and lodging, but when the numbers of customers increased they either shut up their houses or restricted their business to the furnishing of coffee, chocolate, etc., and we could not prevail upon them to provide us with a dinner on any terms.

At the Léon de Oro one afternoon he could get nothing but a glass of liqueur and a few apples. While eating them gloomily he met Captain McMahon of the 60th who took him to the Hotel de Inglaterra which eventually became a sort of officers' mess. At this time, however, its amenities were very limited. He and McMahon went into the dining room at four o'clock and found about thirty people there, nearly all of whom were British officers.

> The table cloth was coarse and dirty; the forks and spoons which were silver looked like pewter; the salt was coarse, brown and almost tasteless; and the apparatus of the table was completed by a mixture of pepper, oil and vinegar which was called 'mustard', although not a particle of that seed had been used in its composition. A decanter filled with a weak red wine, the growth of the province, was placed beside each cover.

They were permitted to drink as much of this 'execrable vino-tinto' as they liked during the three and fourpenny meal of meat, game, fish, poultry and fruit which was eventually placed before them by an evil-looking waiter with a dirty napkin over his shoulder who was damned by the other officers for a stupid scoundrel. But however much wine you drank, Captain Gordon did not think you ran 'the smallest risk of intoxication '. It tasted like a mixture of vinegar and ink.

The food, the Hon. Berkeley Paget of the 7th Hussars thought, was not much better. 'The Spanish cookery does not suit me', he said. 'A touch of garlick I have no objection to, but my breath was taken away when one dish was put on the table which was a sausage as large as a line-of-battleship's main-yard cram full of garlick, a dish of macaroni poisoned with saffron and a salad dressed with lamp-oil.'

In the evenings after dinner, the only public entertainment the town afforded was the theatre where stylised comedies, stories from sacred history, improvised Shakespeare and allegorical pieces of topical allusion were performed without regard to either taste or pleasure. The actors 'get through their parts with much spirit', a member of the audience once remarked, but he thought that this might well have been because they were determined not to be outdone by the prompters who declaimed their lines loud enough for everyone to hear and much louder than the actors did after them.

A popular play for presentation to audiences which included a high proportion of English officers was one in which Spain, represented as a beautiful woman enslaved by the treachery of a French villain, was rescued by the noble efforts of a gallant English hero in a yellow wig. The final scene showed George III and numerous members of his Royal Family embracing Ferdinand who was to marry an English princess. The curtain fell to shouts of '*Viva Ferdinando! Viva Jorge tercero!*'

For most officers one visit to the theatre was as much as they felt inclined to undergo. But evenings in private houses could be even worse. The conversation was conducted in the most formal manner with long rows of men facing long rows of women in large, sparsely furnished rooms, hardly any of which had a fireplace. Card games were played in silence, music was heard to an accompaniment of raucous hawking as the guests, both men and women, abstractedly spat on to the floor. Occasionally sugared biscuits and lemonade were offered or cups of rich chocolate followed by pint tumblers of cold water and preserved fruits, but more often the officers were offered only the damp end of a communal cigar.

Young women were rarely seen, and when permitted to attend a private dance and partner an English officer they were closely watched as they circled the floor with formal grace. Only those officers gracious, kind and patient enough to observe the strict rules of Spanish propriety were liked; the rest were tolerated or ignored. Lady Holland, who had come out with her husband to witness for herself the struggle of the Spanish people she so much admired, noted in her diary that they found the English 'very cold'. 'The ladies praise their complexion, blue eyes and

height of the men,' she added, 'but complain of want of expression in
their countenance and delicacy in the shape of their limbs.' They also
complained of their casual arrogance. 'Some of the Guards', Charles Napier
told his mother, 'are very impertinent and not liked.' And he, himself,
found it difficult to be polite to the 'poor, frippery, little apprentice-
looking people', who were the Spanish gentry. As for the common people
they were to a man '*cruel, dirty, cheating, proud* and *crafty*. They ought to
be exterminated for their treatment of animals, and flogged for laxness.'

'The credulous Spaniards', another officer who also could not get on
with them wrote,

> were accustomed in the streets and in their houses to assemble in parties,
> and whilst one read the *Madrid* or *Corunna Gazette,* which contained more
> of invention than matter of fact, the rest laid down the positions for their
> nominal armies, generally amounting to 200,000 men and the French army
> which they never admitted to exceed 50,000 was always being surrounded
> and annihilated. If the British officers attempted to describe the true state
> they were disbelieved and the Spaniards would only admit as fact such
> intelligence as was acceptable and in their own favour.

Sir David Baird, for his part, thought the whole race a 'disgraceful set'.
On October 23rd he at last received permission to disembark. A Galician
officer riding from Aranjuez by leisurely stages had brought the reluctant
agreement of the Supreme Junta. Even so Baird was asked to send forward
his troops into the interior in detachments of not more than 2,000 men
with intervals between them. The resources of the country would not
permit concentration.

By this time, indeed, Baird himself was beginning to wonder whether
his own resources would permit him to advance at all. The Government
had supplied him with very little coin and the Spaniards were no more
prepared than the Portuguese to accept British Government bills. They
wanted silver dollars, and the rates they charged for carts and draught
animals were exorbitant. Without hard Spanish cash he could not move
his army; and all the hard cash he could manage to raise in Corunna was
6,000 dollars. He felt a personal irritation for he was used to Indian warfare
and he had brought a great deal of luggage, which it seemed he might
have to leave behind.

Eventually the Galician Junta came to his help and with a generosity
as unexpected as it was commendable agreed to lend him a further 92,000
dollars. Some days later John Hookham Frere, appointed British Minister
in Madrid, arrived in the harbour and brought with him £410,000 which
he was empowered to disburse in aid of the national resistance. He left

£40,000 with the army in Corunna before continuing his journey. Sir David also later received 50,000 dollars from the frigate *Tigre* and £8,000 in dollars from Moore who had discovered that the Spaniards' 'dread of paper money' was as great as that of the Portuguese and had written to Charles Stuart, representative with the Supreme Junta in Aranjuez, to say that even if money could only be borrowed at a hundred per cent, he must have it.

With cash enough at last to pay for their transport, Baird's troops began to disembark on October 26th. The Spaniards did not seem pleased to see them. 'It would be premature to judge of the feelings of the Body of the People from what it exhibited in an extreme seaport like this,' one officer said, 'but it would not appear that the arrival of 15,000 English inspires much joy.'

The arrival, however, of 9,000 Spanish troops under General the Marqués de la Romana created a quite different impression. The Marqués was a hero to the people. Three months before his army had been unwillingly performing garrison duties for Napoleon in North Germany, where on the arrival of a British fleet in Göteborg Harbour they had happily dashed on board and sailed away to England. Now they had returned to throw the French out of their homeland. While the troops were disembarked further west and sent to join General Blake's army, Romana himself came ashore at Corunna. He was dragged through the streets in a carriage filled with flowers to the wildly enthusiastic cheers of the populace. He stood up to acknowledge the deafening '*vivas*' which affected him so much he sobbed aloud. Mr. Henry Crabb Robinson, *The Times*'s correspondent in Spain, was not impressed. 'In my eyes', he wrote in his journal, 'Romana looks like a Spanish barber.'

Robinson had been in Corunna since the end of July and at first had been deeply impressed by the patriotism and determination of the Spanish people. 'We need not fear the speedy emancipation of the Capital,' he had written in his first despatch, 'and the compression of the French force within the provinces adjoining Bayonne.' Three months later he was not so optimistic. Sir David Baird was even less so. Although his troops had begun to disembark on October 26th, the last detachment of infantry did not leave the town until November 10th. It was five days before the first detachment of cavalry followed them. By this time Lord Paget, the commander of the cavalry, was as exasperated as Sir David himself.

Paget had been much in the company of Lord and Lady Holland, but he did not trouble to disguise the disdain with which he regarded the Spaniards whom he spoke of as the Hollands' protégés. The Spaniards, for their part, although 'very much struck with his beauty', as Lady Holland put it, thought him a very haughty young man. It was an unfair judgment. He was tall, dignified and rather remote, but he was not arrogant. He had been born in 1768, the eldest of the Earl of Uxbridge's six sons, and he was already a lieutenant-general at the age of forty. Impetuous but shrewd, as brave and determined as his younger brother Edward, he had earned the reputation of being one of the best cavalry officers in the Army. 'To say that he was liked by the soldiers', one of his men once said, 'would convey but a faint idea of his popularity; he was almost idolised.' The respect and affection which his men had for him continued throughout the long and bitter winter. From the first he had need of their unquestioning obedience.

The Galician Junta had not emphasised the difficulties of supply and subsistence in their desolate mountains. Forage was scarce, accommodation in the villages rarely obtainable. In order to spare the horses as much as possible, and allow them time to recover from the effects of confinement during the seven weeks' voyage, the route to Astorga – 180 miles from Corunna along the road to Salamanca – had to be taken in twelve easy stages with two halting days. Even so gentle a pace was too much for some of them. Lady Holland had seen the feverish horses swim ashore in Corunna harbour and on her way south saw several of them hobbling pitifully along behind the main columns. In Betanzos she counted seventeen horses lying dead by the roadside and others, weakened by a sudden change of food from oats and hay to chopped straw and maize, struggling ineffectually to rise to their scabrous legs.

The main body of the cavalry had accordingly not got far beyond Lugo, when on November 22nd Sir David Baird, with four brigades of infantry and three batteries of artillery, came down from the mountains to the Leon plain at Astorga. He was greeted there by the news of the rout of the Army of Galicia under Blake at Espinosa and the defeat of the Army of Estramadura under the Conde de Belveder at Gamonal. Marshal Soult, he was informed, was already at Reinosa only a hundred miles to the north-east and Marshal Lefebvre even closer on the banks of the Carrion. He believed that they might be endeavouring to close in on the town of Leon less than fifty miles away. Baird decided to call a halt at Astorga and prepare to retreat to Corunna if his fears were justified. He sent a message south to Moore at Salamanca to tell him of his decision and his danger. That night Cornet Laroche of the 15th Hussars was galloping for all he was worth back along the road to Corunna, with orders to halt all the troops he should meet on the road.

'We have no business here', Moore wrote in his diary the following day. 'But being here it would never do to abandon the Spaniards without a struggle.'

He had been in Salamanca for ten days now and had become increasingly worried by the perils of his predicament. Despite the alarming news from the Spanish armies, Hope and Baird had both been given discretionary orders to join him with all speed but he considered a junction 'very precarious'. He had less than 17,000 men with him and a single battery of light guns. Hope with the rest of his artillery and all his cavalry was still far to the south beyond the Sierra de Gredos. Baird's force, straggling for miles between the passes of the Cantabrian mountains and Astorga, was even farther way to the north. The intelligence he received of French movements was always vague and sometimes contradictory; the information he was given of Spanish movements was misleading and negligible. That the French had occupied Valladolid and were concentrating in force along the banks of the Carrion he knew, but what the Spaniards were doing he could only guess at. 'I am in communication with no one Spanish army,' he complained in an angry letter to Mr. Hookham Frere, the British Government's Envoy who had now arrived in Madrid, 'nor am I acquainted with the intentions of the Spanish Government or any of its Generals. The imbecility of the Spanish Government exceeds belief. The goodwill of the inhabitants, whatever that may be, is of little use while there exists no ability to bring it into action.' And even now, when events had proved the necessity for a supreme commander of the Spanish armies, no appointment to that essential command had been made.

As for the Spanish troops, the reports he received of them were uniformly depressing. One report, characteristic of many, was sent on to him from Madrid by Lord William Bentinck, one of those few British representatives with the Spaniards who saw the country's dilemma in a clear light undimmed by the befogging confidence of Spanish officials. The report referred to the Army of Castile, the strength of which was officially given as more than 11,000 men:

> But to form any idea of its composition, it is absolutely necessary to have seen it. It is a complete mass of miserable peasantry, without clothing, without organisation, and with few officers that deserve the name. The General and principal officers have not the least confidence in their troops; and what is worse, the men have no confidence in themselves. This is not an exaggerated picture, it is a true portrait.

The main hope for the Spanish people, Lord William observed, must in these circumstances be the English army.

But this was a view which Moore could not accept. His instructions from the Government had been 'to co-operate with the Spanish armies in the expulsion of the French' and not to act alone. 'The British Army, I hope,' he replied to Lord William, 'will do all which can be expected from their numbers: but the safety of Spain depends upon the union of its inhabitants, their enthusiasm in their cause, and in their firm and devoted determination to die rather than submit.' Of this determined resistance, Moore could find no evidence. On November 24th he wrote to inform Lord Castlereagh of his predicament:

> The enthusiasm of which we heard so much nowhere appears.... I am at this moment in no communication with any of their generals. I am ignorant of their plans or those of their Government.... I cannot calculate the power of a whole people determined and enthusiastic, if persons are brought forward with ability to direct it, but at present nothing of this kind appears, and yet I see no other chance Spain has of resistance. We are here by ourselves, left to manage the best way we can, without communication with any other army; no knowledge of the strength or positions of the Enemy, but what we can pick up in a country where we are strangers, and in complete ignorance of the plans or wishes of the Spanish Government.

Two days later he had learned nothing new. 'I am in a scrape from which God knows how I am to extricate myself ', he told his brother in a worried, rambling letter which clearly shows his deep anxiety. 'I sleep little; it is now only five in the morning, and I have concluded since I got up, this long letter.'

His anxiety and sleeplessness showed in his manner and in the features of his pale face. Never a patient man with those whom he took to be incompetent or verbose, his reserve and brusqueness were now strongly accentuated. Visiting officers spoke of his sarcasm and disdain. Spanish noblemen, unused to so haughty a response to their own proud overtures, found him, so Lady Holland said, 'sulky and repulsive'. His staff well aware of his mood and temperament, took care to keep him secure from the intrusions of those whom he was likely to find distasteful; but they were not always successful and on more than one occasion there was an embarrassing incident at dinner in the dining room of the Palacio de San Boal when a guest irritated the General. A disdainful look, a cold reply, a faint subconscious gesture of scorn for a moment disturbed the watching officers of his staff and forced them to exercise a careful tact as they steered the conversation into less dangerous waters. They performed this duty willingly. Their General's inability to conceal his annoyance and his sudden accesses of haughty reserve were the only faults, if faults they were, in a character they admired to the point of veneration. They loved him and served him devotedly.

They were all distinguished men – his five aides-de-camp particularly so. Two of them, Captain Burrard, son of Sir Harry Burrard, and Captain the Hon. Henry Percy, son of the Earl of Beverley, were promising officers; the other three were already remarkable ones. The eldest, Colonel Thomas Graham, had not joined the army until he was over thirty. He had at that time conceived a hatred for revolutionary France when his beautiful wife had died of consumption in the Mediterranean and her coffin, on its return from Toulouse, had been broken open by drunken soldiers who thought it contained arms for their enemies. Graham, created Lord Lynedoch after the war, was very close to Moore and as a good linguist and tactful diplomat was extremely useful to him. He died, a full general, at the age of ninety-five.

George Napier also became a general. Brother of William, whose history was later to become one of the great epic narratives of war, and of Charles, commanding officer of the 50th Regiment, he was the great-great-grandson of Charles II and Louise de Kéroualle, the son of Lady Sarah Lennox and second cousin to Charles James Fox. He was one of those rare young men whose astonishingly good looks, influential family connections, and great talents left him charming and unspoiled. Moore was devoted to him and he to Moore.

Perhaps the most distinguished of all these exceptional young men was Henry Hardinge, later to become Field-Marshal Viscount Hardinge and the Duke of Wellington's successor as Commander-in-Chief of the British Army. He was now twenty-four, and had been chosen by Moore for his staff solely on account of his gifts and outstanding record as a regimental officer.

It was an unusual method of selecting aides-de-camp and one which other generals, whose staffs were comprised of relatives and the sons of influential friends, might well have followed. Moore himself, of course, was repeatedly being asked to take on to his staff young officers whose capabilities were unknown. He did not always refuse. While at Salamanca he received a letter from Lady Hester Stanhope who asked him to accept as another aide-de-camp her 'little brother James'. Moore did not really need a sixth aide. But, he confessed in reply, he could refuse her nothing. 'He must get the Commander-in-Chief's leave to come to Spain', he said. 'He may then join me. He will, however, come too late; I shall already be beaten.'

It was his constant fear. Only his staff knew how hard he worked to avert what he so often now believed to be inevitable disaster. He was up before four o'clock every morning and while they still slept he lit the fire in his room and the candles on his writing table and worked alone until eight. It was a long, bare and narrow room with a window overlooking the square. In the middle, between arm-chairs ranged along the sides of the room in a single row, were several tables covered with maps and papers. After four or sometimes five hours' writing, he joined his staff for breakfast. Then he received the generals and anyone else who had business to discuss with him, and afterwards returned again to his solitary work. He wrote every letter himself and took care to compose the official ones well, for he was a man of scrupulous method and fastidious taste.

For an hour or two before dinner he rode about the town and the camps outside it, asking questions, giving advice, checking with his own sharply observant eyes the reports that came to him. 'He was a refined, somewhat pallid and interesting looking man,' a commissary who had been summoned to report on the victualling of the regiments, said of him, 'with *a je ne sais quoi* of melancholy in his expression. He was grave but courteous and asked me how everything was going.' When he returned for dinner there were usually between fourteen and twenty officers in the dining room. The meal was always good and varied, but he himself ate little and chose the plainest food, seldom drinking more than three or four glasses of wine with it, for after dinner he went back to his room with his Military Secretary to work again until ten.

He was becoming convinced now that he would have to retire from Salamanca and had decided that he would do so as soon as General Hope joined him with the guns and the cavalry, provided that by then no improvement had been shown in the Spanish attitude. 'It was not expected', he told Hookham Frere who was strongly pressing him to use his men more daringly, that his small army should have

to cope alone with the whole force of France: as auxiliaries they were to aid a people who were believed to be enthusiastic and determined and prepared for resistance. It becomes, therefore, a question of whether the British army should remain to be attacked in its turn, or should retire from a country where the contest, from whatever circumstances, is becoming unequal.

The following evening the question was decided for him. Having ridden nearly 500 miles in six days, Charles Vaughan, secretary to Mr. Stuart, representative with the Supreme Junta at Aranjuez, galloped into Salamanca and there handed to Moore despatches which the General considered made his immediate withdrawal essential.

On November 23rd, Vaughan had been on the south bank of the Ebro at Tudela, when Castaños and Palafox, commanding the only undefeated Spanish armies between Moore and the French, had been overwhelmed there. It was the second serious disaster which had befallen the Spanish armies within a fortnight. It left his own incomplete force of 17,000 men to combat alone a French army which the estimate of agents put at 80,000 but which was, in fact, considerably stronger. That evening Moore wrote to Sir David Baird:

> It certainly was much my wish to have run great risks in aid of the people of Spain; but, after this second proof of how little they are able to do for themselves . . . I see no right to expect from them much greater exertions; at any rate we should be overwhelmed before they could be prepared. I see no chance of our being able to form a junction; as certainly at Burgos the French have a corps which will now move forward. I have, therefore, determined to retreat upon Portugal with the corps I have here; and, if possible, with Hope's corps, if by forced marches he can join me. I wish you to fall back on Corunna.

He closed the letter and picked up his pen again to write to Hope:

> I have determined to give the thing up and retire. A junction with Baird is out of the question, and with you, perhaps, problematical.... This is a cruel determination for me to make – I mean to retreat: but I hope you will think the circumstances such as demand it.

Hope did think the circumstances demanded it, and so did Baird. But few of the other general officers agreed with them. They had come into Spain to fight the French and were now running away before they had even seen them. They went so far as to show their disapproval of Moore's decision at a meeting which he called at the palace in order to give them their instructions. Moore rebuked them sternly. He had not, he said, called the meeting to ask the generals for their advice or opinion. The decision was entirely his own responsibility; he only required that they should 'immediately prepare for carrying it into effect'.

The discontent was silenced, but throughout the army the disappointment and sense of betrayal went deep. For days there had been rumours that the army was preparing to go back to Portugal and the men had constantly been asking their officers to deny these rumours as they themselves had indignantly denied them when any Spaniard had suggested they might be true. Now they had been confirmed. The men returned to their quarters in the town, shamefaced and angry. 'It is not surprising', one of them said, sympathising with the Spaniards' unconcealed contempt, 'that our allies should have formed unfavourable opinions of our intentions from witnessing the indecision of our commanders.' 'The suspicions of the Spaniards are aroused and no wonder', another wrote. 'The Spanish magistrates had orders, they say, "to assist the British advancing, but not retiring". They are right.'

Stuart and Hookham Frere were both aghast at Moore's decision. Stuart, while admitting it did not become him to hazard an opinion on the military aspects of the matter, told Moore that the retrograde movement was very likely to produce an effect in Madrid, 'not less serious than the most decisive victory on the part of the Enemy'. Frere was much more forceful. Indeed so certain was he that Moore was committing an error of the gravest significance that he took a step which was soon to have a catastrophic effect on their already strained relationship. While Moore, in the phrase which he committed to his diary on November 30th, was 'making every preparation to retreat', Napoleon was advancing towards Madrid. Immediately after his armies had smashed the resistance they had met at Tudela on the Ebro, he crossed the river himself and advanced on the snow-covered Sierra de Guadarrama. His advance guard was checked at the narrow pass of Somosierra where 12,000 Spanish troops, sent out hurriedly from Madrid, were barring the way to the capital. But, as the mist fell down from the heights, disguising their movements, the Polish lancers of the Imperial Guard charged the guns in the defile and overthrew them, toppling thousands of ill-trained Spanish troops down into the plains of New Castile. Madrid was left open to Napoleon's advance. On the last day of November, the advance cavalry of the Imperial Guard came into view of the city.

On the bitterly cold night of that same day, General Hope's men, tired after a long day's march, slept in square without piling arms. During the day French dragoons had got within twenty miles of their right flank as they hurried north to join forces with Moore at Ciudad Rodrigo. Hope knew how essential it was that he should reach Moore before the French cavalry, streaming across the plain of New Castile, should discover his whereabouts. He did not spare his men and horses. In the first thirty-six hours of December he marched forty-seven miles to Peñaranda where the artillery horses were so exhausted that six guns were abandoned and buried and their crews split up to help pull other guns. The pace slowed down after Peñaranda and on reaching Alba de Tormes, Hope received orders not to continue his movement to Ciudad Rodrigo but to turn north to Salamanca where Moore was still in his original position, having so far only sent back the heavy ammunition and the sick under an escort provided by the 5th Battalion of the 60th.

For at Salamanca the news seemed daily more hopeful. On December 3rd Brigadier-General Augustin Bueno and Don Ventura Escalante, Captain General of the Kingdom of Leon, arrived at Moore's headquarters from Aranjuez with a letter from Don Martin de Garay, the secretary of the Supreme Junta, authorising them to discuss with Moore a plan of

action for a new campaign and a combined march to the relief of Madrid.
Apart from this hopeful evidence of the Spaniards' determination to resist
now that Napoleon was so close to their capital, the two generals brought
with them encouraging information regarding their country's armies.
Castaños had escaped intact from Tudela with his Andalusian army of
about 25,000 men, and was just north of Madrid; General Heredia had
rallied 10,000 men of the Estramaduran Army at Segovia; San Juan had
another 12,000 in the Guadarramas; levies from Andalusia and the Castiles
were coming into Madrid every day and already numbered about 10,000
men. There were thus about 60,000 determined men still under arms,
and, if Moore joined with his 20,000 British troops, they would be more
than a match for the 20,000 French troops concentrating on Madrid.
Napoleon, they insisted, had no more than 80,000 troops in Spain all
told.

Moore listened to the excitedly enthusiastic generals with caution and
reserve. He had been misled too often now by Spanish promise and
Spanish estimates to treat them with unquestioning respect. But the
emissaries of the Supreme Junta – although, in his subsequently expressed
opinion, 'weak old men, or rather women' – could not be ignored. There
was other evidence too that the Spaniards might be arousing themselves
at last. He had recently received a letter from the Marqués de la Romana
informing him that he was at the head of a considerable force in Leon
and that although his men were not well equipped they were in good
heart and anxious to fight. The people as well as the troops, Moore dared
to hope, were becoming imbued with new spirit. An example of this he
recorded in his diary: Lord Proby, confidential agent he had sent out from
Salamanca to try to obtain news of the French,

> was at Fordillas when a patrol of French cavalry came into the town; they
> stayed some time. Every man in the town knew that Proby was there. He
> had been there two days, yet not a man betrayed him, and when the cavalry
> left and he came into the streets they all testified their satisfaction and
> declared that, though they had no arms, yet they would have died rather
> than have allowed him to be taken. They are fine people, and it will only be
> for want of men of ability starting up to direct them if they do not succeed.

From Madrid as well there came reports of a people determined to die
rather than surrender. Brigadier-General Charles Stewart, commanding
the cavalry in Hope's force, had now got through to Salamanca. He had
made a detour through Madrid and had witnessed for himself that 'all
were united in one enthusiastic resolution to conquer or perish... A huge
trench was already drawn round the entire circumference of the city;

numerous outworks were begun; and men and women of all ranks were labouring incessantly for their completion.' Stewart, like so many other officers of the army, was annoyed that, despite Moore's knowledge of the promised resistance of Madrid and his professed sympathy with the unled Spanish people, he should nevertheless exhibit 'no signs of any alterations in his previous resolutions'. He had not yet made a movement from Salamanca but when he did it would certainly not be against the French. He 'explicitly stated to me', Stewart wrote with indignation, 'that he had come to a final determination to retreat. . . reasoning in conversation, as he reasoned in his letters, with a decided leaning to the gloomy side of the picture. He spoke warmly in condemnation of the Spanish Government, and of the nation generally.' 'The die is cast', Stewart told his half-brother Lord Castlereagh in a letter which warned him of Moore's unalterable decision to retreat. 'Would to heaven we had the hero of Vimiero at our head now!'

The fact was that Moore, in spite of his admiration for their occasional acts of heroism, was sceptical of the ability of the Spanish people, with little more than pride and courage on their side, to fulfil their promises. In addition he knew that the leaders of the people were blinded by a self-justificatory confidence in adversity which was, and remains, a characteristic feature of the Spanish temperament.

He had good cause to doubt, for instance, that the Supreme Junta had any real reason for supposing that the active force of their armies numbered 60,000 men. There was nothing so easy, as he told Stuart, 'as for the Junta, with their pens, to form armies'. He had cause also to doubt that Romana's 25,000 men in Leon were in reality anything more than '5,000 fugitives from Blake, without arms, clothing, stores or ammunition'. His doubt was justified. While the old generals Bueno and Escalante were still at Salamanca, imparting the Supreme Junta's doubtful information and discussing their impossible objectives, Colonel Graham, who had been on a mission to the Spanish armies, came into the room and Moore introduced him to them. Graham knew, which they apparently did not, that Napoleon had already crossed the Guadarramas, that the army with which they were proposing to defend the Somosierra Pass no longer existed, and that the army which they had described as being at Segovia had long since retreated headlong from it.

It was then with particular irritation that Moore read on December 5th a letter addressed to him by Hookham Frere from Madrid. Frere, who had been one of the Foreign Secretary's closest friends ever since they had been boys together at Eton, was amusing, lazy, untidy, clever, sensitive and extremely emotional. He knew Spain well and from 1802 to 1804 he had been Minister in Madrid. Now that he was there again, he felt certain that the Spanish setbacks were only slight and temporary and that Moore's behaviour was both timid and reprehensible. He had described the defeat of the Estramaduran Army under the Conde de Belveder as the 'unlucky affair of the 10th near Burgos', which had 'not created any visible degree of uneasiness or discouragement in the minds of the leading persons here'. The news that Moore had decided to retreat appalled him. 'I cannot forbear representing to you in the strongest possible manner', Frere had written, 'the propriety, not to say the necessity, of supporting the determination of the Spanish people, by all the means which have been entrusted to you for that purpose.' A retreat at this stage would be disastrous. Madrid was showing every sign of fanatical determination. 30,000 citizens and peasants were under arms. Barricades and batteries were being erected all over the city. It would be unforgivable to leave the brave Spaniards to their fate.

The tone of the letter was so forceful that Moore took it to be insulting. But while he might have forgiven Frere, who wrote it under the strain of great excitement and anxiety, he could not forgive the choice of messenger.

Colonel Venault de Charmilly was a French emigré of unprepossessing appearance and doubtful honesty, who had lived in England for some years and had married Lord Dufferin's sister. While in London he had been successively a coal merchant, a distiller and a money-lender, but bankruptcy had obliged him to forgo a business career for a life of intrigue and adventure. Moore had already met him when he had called at the British Headquarters on his way to Madrid, where he had unsuccessfully tried to obtain a cavalry appointment from the Junta. The General had taken an immediate dislike to him. He was self-opinionated, vain, pretentious and ingratiating.

Now that he had persuaded Frere to entrust him with this confidential mission, Moore felt less inclined to like him than ever. When his presence at Salamanca was announced Moore refused at first to receive him and asked one of his aides to collect Frere's letter from him and bring it up to his room. Charmilly refused to hand it over to the aide-de-camp and told him that he had undertaken to deliver it personally to the General and would wait until Sir John was at liberty to see him.

'After ten minutes', Charmilly wrote afterwards, 'Sir John Moore came out and received me coolly.'

Moore read the letter and then questioned Charmilly about it. The Colonel vividly described the patriotic zeal in Madrid, confirming General Stewart's report. All the inhabitants of the city were in arms, he said, and had united with the troops. Peasants were flocking to the capital; people worked by the light of flambeaux; the streets were broken up and the stones carried to the tops of the houses. Sir John listened to all this 'without uttering a word which could indicate his thoughts'. Then, Colonel Charmilly continued,

> after having talked of other matters, he said, more kindly than in the beginning of the conversation, 'You must be very much fatigued, and want to rest yourself; I thank you for your zeal; have you good quarters?' I answered that I was at the house of one of the first merchants of Salamanca in the square. 'Then,' said he, 'I am very busy to-night, but I shall be glad to see you at eleven o'clock to-morrow morning.'

So Charmilly took his leave and retired to bed, but not before he had heard the 'important merchant' state in his room, 'when taking some refreshments, his opinion, as well as of all the people of Salamanca upon the disaster of the retreat'.

Moore, when he was alone, thought over what Frere had written and what Charmilly had told him. A few hours before he had received a similar plea from Don Thomas de Morla and the Prince of Castelfranco, the military leaders of the newly created Junta of Defence in Madrid, who asked him to distract Napoleon's attention from the capital by manoeuvring on the flanks of the French army. They had got 40,000 men for the defence of Madrid, they said, and only needed the help of a manoeuvrable army outside it.

Moore's every instinct told him to give way and take his little army to the help of the patriots, but his reason held him back. How long, he afterwards confessed to wondering, could this sudden enthusiasm last? How much could the Spaniards, with their armies broken on every side, really accomplish? How far was he justified in risking the army entrusted to his care – the only British army in the field – and leading it against an enemy whose strength he could only guess? He had constantly in mind his original instructions to support the Spanish armies. No one had expected him to fight the French alone. Within the last day or so he had had those instructions repeated. 'You will keep in mind', Lord Castlereagh had written from Downing Street, 'that the British army is sent by His Majesty as an *auxiliary* force, to support the Spanish nation against the attempts of Buonaparte to effect their subjugation.'

All that evening he thought his problem over. For days now he had thought of little else, and 'it was easy', General Stewart, the most actively critical of his senior officers, thought, 'to perceive marks of that gloom which at this time overshadowed' his mind. It was 'manifest that a fear of responsibility neutralised his talents and warped his judgment'. Before midnight, however, he had come to a firm decision. He had resolved to

Sir John Moore by Sir Thomas Lawrence

Alexander Mackenzie Fraser, from an
engraving by Henry Meyer after a
painting by Richard Cosway

The Hon. John Hope from a
contemporary engraving

Lord Paget, later Marquess of Anglesey
by Sir Thomas Lawrence

Jean-Baptiste Franceski from a
contemporary engraving

Sir David Baird by Sir David Wilkie

Lord William Bentinck from an
engraving after a painting by
Sir Thomas Lawrence

Petro Caro y Suredo, Marqués de la
Romano from an engraving by
A. Cardon

Alexandre Berthier from a
contemporary engraving

Nicolas Jean de Dieu Soult, Duke of
Dalmatia from an engraving by
Henri Grévedon

William Carr Beresford by
Sir Thomas Lawrence

'The Convention of Cintra, a Portuguese Gambol for the Amusement of John Bull'
engraved from a drawing by G. Woodward, 1809

'Soldiers on the March' from a caricature by Thomas Rowlandson

countermand the retreat. Immediately he wrote to Baird, who had already
fallen back fifty miles to Villafranca, and then to Lord Castlereagh.

In both communications his fears and doubts were apparent. He made
no secret of the fact that he thought the sudden Spanish resistance might
well have come too late. 'There is, however, no saying,' he told Baird,
'and I feel myself the more obliged to give it a trial, as Mr. Frere has made
a formal representation which I received this evening. All this appears
very strange and unsteady.' Before dawn on the 16th detailed orders for
Baird's advance were given. The cavalry were to advance without delay
to Zamora, the infantry to Benavente. 'I mean to proceed,' he warned
with a graphic imagery which was to be remembered for ever,

> bridle in hand; for if the bubble bursts and Madrid falls we shall have a run
> for it. Both you and me, though we may look big, and determined to get
> everything forward, yet we must never lose sight of this, that at any
> moment affairs may take the turn that will render it necessary to retreat.

The decision nevertheless was taken at last. Orders were prepared for
an advance on Valladolid behind a screen of cavalry. The Headquarters
staff were woken before dawn, informed of the General's plan and given
their numerous instructions.

The army heard the news with delight. 'But a few hours ago,' Charles
Stewart wrote,

> and every face looked blank and woebegone; men did their duty indeed –
> attended to their horses and accoutrements – and performed all the other
> offices which their stations required, mechanically – but now all was life
> and activity, and military duties were executed, not only without murmur
> but with apparent satisfaction.

All the aides-de-camp, except Captain Percy, were out on duty when
punctually at eleven o'clock, as arranged the previous evening, Colonel
Charmilly presented himself at the Palace for the second time. Captain
Percy told him that the General had gone to his room straight after breakfast
and that, as he was so busy, he had given orders not to be disturbed.

'I advise you to call again at one o'clock,' Percy said, 'very likely the
General will have finished writing, and as he generally rides at that time,
you will see him before he goes out.'

Charmilly returned at half past one and was told that the General had
not once been out of his room since he had last called. 'I suppose', Percy
suggested, 'that he means to finish his despatches before he rides, as there
is a King's Messenger going to England to-night.'

To Captain Percy's surprise this suggestion seemed to strike Charmilly as an appalling one. He became extremely agitated and said that it was essential for him to see the General before he finished his despatch, as he himself had a despatch of 'very great consequence' to hand to him. Captain Percy agreed to take Colonel Charmilly to Major Colborne whose room led into the General's. With great reluctance the Military Secretary went in, and returned instantly to tell Charmilly that the General would see him.

Moore was already furious. Unable to contain his anger, he had risen from his chair and was at the door when the Frenchman walked in.

'What does this mean, Colonel Charmilly?' he said in a voice breaking with anger. 'A letter from Mr. Frere! And why did you not give it to me last night?'

Charmilly said his instructions were not to hand it over for some hours after having delivered his first letter.

'Sir John Moore took the letter from me with great impatience for which I was not prepared', Colonel Charmilly wrote in an account of the interview in which he thought it best to indicate the General's furious words by asterisks. 'I looked at him with astonishment. On my attempting to speak he immediately said, "Sir, will you be so good as to go near the fire, and let me read that letter."'

He broke the seal. The few words were soon read. He marched across the room to face Charmilly.

'Do you know the contents of this letter ?' he demanded.

'Yes, sir,' said Charmilly.

His one excuse, his possible means of escape from Moore's anger were gone. For Frere's letter asked that, in the event of Moore rejecting the demands contained in his previous one and refusing to go to the help of the people of Madrid (an event which Frere did 'not wish to presuppose'), he should let Colonel Charmilly express his views before a meeting of the other generals of the army. To Moore this was not merely the indiscretion of a civilian unacquainted with the management of military affairs; it was not merely an insult; it was an enticement to mutiny. And he dealt with it accordingly. He ordered the provost-marshal to expel this outrageous Frenchman from the camp without delay. He sat down to reply to Mr. Frere:

> I shall abstain from any remark upon the two letters from you delivered to me last night and this morning by Colonel Charmilly, or on the message which accompanied them.... I hope as we have but one interest, the public welfare, though we may occasionally see it in different aspects, that this will not disturb the harmony that should subsist between us.... I certainly

at first did feel and expressed much indignation at a person like Colonel Charmilly being made the channel of a communication of that sort from you to me. Those feelings are at an end; and I dare say they never will be excited towards you again.

If Mr. Charmilly is your friend, it was, perhaps, natural for you to employ him; but I have prejudices against all that class; and it is impossible for me to put any trust in him. I shall, therefore, thank you not to employ him any more in any communication with me.

He addressed the cover in his thin, trailing handwriting, and turned his mind to more important matters.

Now that his anger had cooled he felt encouraged. The days of uncertainty were over. For better or worse he had made up his mind and that in itself was a comfort of a sort. As soon as Baird joined him he would move forward. He sent Colonel Graham with instructions to find out exactly what was happening in Madrid and gave him a letter which he was to hand to Thomas de Morla and the Prince of Castelfranco when he arrived there. Graham, however, had only got as far as Talavera when he was given bitter news. 'It seems that on the 3rd', he wrote to tell Moore,

Castelfranco and Morla made some sort of agreement with the French, who on the day before got possession of the Retiro and Prado of Madrid. They are suspected of treason in this proceeding, having refused to admit the troops under St. Juan and Heredia who were at the gates on this side, and whose presence, it is asserted, would have enabled the citizens to have defended the town.

The unfortunate General San Juan was murdered by his enraged fellow-countrymen who blamed him for this latest disgrace; and on December 4th Napoleon entered Madrid.

Six days later Colonel Graham arrived back in Salamanca with the distressing news. Although he had been obliged to make a detour to avoid a French patrol which had nearly captured him, he had overtaken his despatch and reported to the General who knew nothing of it. Moore was saddened but not dismayed. He had half expected that Madrid would fall. Only the night before he had committed to his diary his fear that the 'courage of the populace of Madrid may fail; at any rate they may not be able to resist. In short in a moment things may be as bad as ever.'

But, although the Spaniards had shown themselves once more incapable of defending themselves, he would still do his best to help them. With his small army he could not hope to defeat Napoleon in battle, but at least by striking out to the east he might be able to cut across his

communications with France and force the Emperor to turn back to shake
the British off. It seemed certain that the French did not yet know where
he was, and that they believed he might be falling back on Portugal. An
officer, sent to patrol the bank of the Carrion, reported that the French
had evacuated Valladolid. If he could himself reach Valladolid unobserved
and push across the Castilian plain beyond the Carrion, Napoleon would
have to turn back from Madrid and recross the Sierra de Guadarrama.
Having drawn his enemy across the mountains, Moore himself would
have to turn back. He would have to run for his life to the sea; but he
would have given the Spaniards a breathing space.

No one knew better than he the dangerous risk he was running, but
there was at least a chance that he might succeed. 'And whilst there is
that,' he wrote on December 10th to Lord Castlereagh, 'I think myself
bound to run all risks to support it.'

The following morning he was handed another letter from Mr. Frere
who had not yet heard of this decision:

> After the representations which have been made to you from other
> quarters, I can hardly hope that a further remonstrance on my part can
> produce any effect; when high military rank and authority, and the
> influence of persons whom I am told you honour with your private esteem
> have been found unavailing.... But this much I must say, that if the British
> army had been sent abroad with the express purpose of doing the utmost
> possible mischief to the Spanish cause, with the single exception of not
> firing a shot against their troops, they would, according to the measures
> now announced as about to be pursued, have completely fulfilled their
> purpose.

Moore laid the letter aside and did not answer it. He continued with
his preparations to advance.

5

Salamanca to Sahagun

'If only these 20,000 were 100,000! If only more English mothers could feel the horrors of war!'

Napoleon Buonaparte

ON THE MORNING of December 11th the advance from Salamanca began. It was a clear, bright morning and the ground underfoot was hard with frost as the men marched across the bare plain north-east towards Valladolid. They moved in two columns. The men of the left-hand column made for Toro, where Lord Paget with Sir David Baird's cavalry from Corunna was waiting for them. The right-hand column made for Alaejos and Tordesillas with a cavalry screen provided by Charles Stewart. For the whole of that day the troops moved across the bleak plateau, seeing for hours on end no sign of habitation or even of life. The few trees seemed stunted. There were no birds in the air. Occasionally they passed the poor shack of a peasant, its low mud walls the colour of a grey winter's sky, a thin stream of smoke from a chaff and cow-dung fire drifting above the thatched roof. The enemy was nowhere in sight.

But on the following day Captain Dashwood, aide-de-camp to General Stewart, walked into the village of Rueda wearing the brown cloak and . broad-brimmed hat of a Spanish peasant. He found there a French cavalry patrol and a detachment of infantry, and counted their numbers. There seemed about eighty men in all. The cavalry were from the 22nd Chasseurs of General Franceski's cavalry division.

After dark the 18th Light Dragoons surrounded Rueda and closed in quietly. A little after midnight they charged into the village. Eighteen Frenchmen were killed and thirty-five taken prisoner. The first engagement of the campaign was a brilliant success. The examination of the prisoners showed that they had been completely unaware of the British army's position and movements. The French command, they said, was still under the impression that Moore was retreating to Portugal.

So far all was going well. On December 13th Moore himself left Salamanca for Alaejos, while Stewart's cavalry pushed on through Tordesillas and on the northern bank of the Douro linked up with Lord

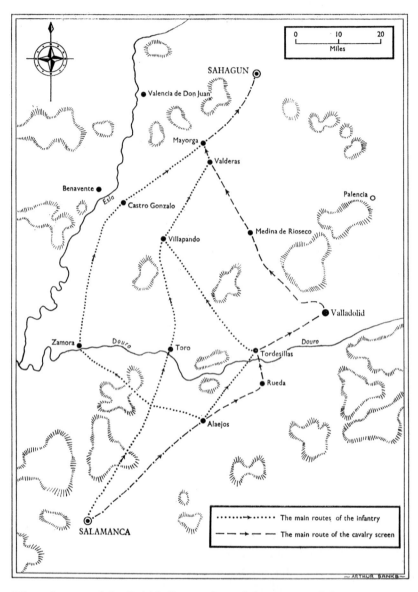

The advance of the British Forces from Salamanca to Sahagun

Paget's cavalry trotting westwards from Toro having seen no sign of the enemy. The army continued its advance towards Valladolid in good spirits. The roads were slippery with frost, and the horses could scarcely keep on their legs; but the air was bright and clear and the sky still blue. 'We were marching fast,' a soldier remembered, 'but we were getting after the French at last and we did not mind it.' On December 15th the pace quickened and the stages became longer. The direction of the advance was due north now and Valladolid was no longer the army's first objective.

For at Alaejos Moore had been given information which had induced him to change his whole plan. A few days before a French officer had ridden into the little village of Valdestillos near Segovia. He was un-escorted but this had not prevented him from behaving in an insolent manner to the unfriendly villagers, and in particular to the postmaster, who had, in accordance with the implacable code of Spanish peasant behaviour, arranged to have him murdered. The villagers stripped the body and emptied the contents of the sabretache, which were offered for sale to a British officer, Captain Waters, who, having been sent to Valdestillos to obtain intelligence about French movements, agreed to buy them for twenty dollars.

It was a purchase of inestimable value. The contents of the sabretache included a despatch from Marshal Berthier in Madrid to Marshal Soult at Saldaña on the Carrion. Captain Waters read the despatch and raced back with it to General Stewart who saw immediately, as he afterwards wrote, that the contents were of vital importance and 'lost no time in forwarding them to Headquarters'.

Soult was informed by Berthier that with his two infantry divisions, commanded by Merle and Mermet, and the four cavalry regiments of Franceski's division he was strong enough to march straight ahead from Saldaña and to take Leon, Zamora, and Benavente. There were no troops to oppose him in the whole of Leon, as the British, who had last been heard of at Salamanca and near the Escorial, were in full retreat towards Lisbon. Lefebvre's corps was at Talavera making south-west for Badajos; Bessières was pursuing the remnants of General Castaños's army across the upper Tagus towards the Mediterranean coast at Valencia; Mortier's corps was in northern Aragon on its way to help in the siege of Saragossa; Junot, whose leading division had reached Villonia, was on his way to Burgos. 'His Majesty', the despatch ended, 'is in the best of health. The city of Madrid is quite tranquil; the shops and theatres are open again. You would never suppose that our first addresses to the place had been emphasised by 4,000 cannon balls.'

A quick glance at the document was sufficient to indicate the opportunity which was now presented to the British army. Marshal Soult with less than 18,000 men was only a hundred miles away to the north on the upper reaches of the Carrion. And he was unsupported there. Junot was marching towards him but he was not yet across the Ebro. The other French forces in Spain were far away to the south in Madrid, in Estramadura and in Valencia; and far away to the east in Aragon. If Moore could join Baird and attack Soult on the Carrion before Junot came up in support, he could feel confident of winning a great victory. But he must be quick. The news of the attack on the French cavalry patrol in Rueda would be sure to reach Madrid soon, and then Napoleon would begin to assemble his forces for an assault on the impudent British who had come so far within his grasp. There could, in addition, no longer be any doubt that the numbers of Napoleon's forces in Spain were nearer 300,000 than the 80,000 which had formerly been supposed.

Within a few hours of reading Berthier's despatch, Moore had issued new orders. An officer was sent galloping north to Baird with instructions to halt his eastward movement and to bring his men down to join the rest of the army at Mayorga; other orders went out to his own leading divisions to proceed due north to meet them there. Moore's infantry crossed the Douro at Zamora and Toro, with a cavalry screen fanning out as far to the east as Valladolid. Several French cavalry patrols from Franceski's division were cut off; and a colonel and more than a hundred dragoons were captured. A squadron of the 8th Hussars galloped into Valladolid and passed within a few miles of Palencia.

The infantry, in dense columns marching well and rapidly, closed in towards Mayorga. The rate of march seemed faster every hour. At each halt the men threw themselves to the frozen ground and fell instantly asleep. But at the sergeant's shout they got up and 'staggered on', a rifleman of the 95th reported, 'looking neither to the right nor to the left'. The weather had become bitterly cold and it had begun to snow. On the evening of December 19th the 15th Hussars led Baird's troops into Mayorga. It had been snowing for some time and they were cold and hungry and exhausted. They had been eleven hours on the march and now waited in heavy snow for another hour while the quartermasters arranged their billets. It continued snowing all night, and in the morning, when the ground was covered to a depth of nearly ten inches, Moore's men, dragging their feet through the heavy drifts, came into the town from the south and the army was united at last.

Before pushing on together to Sahagun, Moore regrouped his units. He formed four infantry divisions, two independent light brigades, and a single cavalry division. He gave the 1st infantry division to Baird, the 2nd to Hope, the 3rd to Fraser and the reserve to Edward Paget. Karl Alten was appointed to command one of the light brigades and Robert Craufurd the other. Lord Paget was to command the cavalry division with one brigade under John Slade and the other under Charles Stewart.* There were about 25,000 infantry in all, with 2,450 cavalry and 1,297 artillery manning 66 guns. Any hope, however, that the Marqués de la Romana would be able to provide the additional 20,000 men that he had originally promised was gone. For a liaison officer reported that the Spanish army at Leon, which was in a 'completely inefficient state', was unlikely to be able to provide any worthwhile assistance to the British campaign:

> It is morally impossible that the Spanish troops can stand before a line of French infantry. A portion of, at least one third of, the Spanish muskets will not explode; and a French soldier will load and fire his piece with precision three times before a Spaniard can fire his twice. Men, however brave, cannot stand against such odds; as to charging with the bayonet, if their arms were fit for the purpose, the men, though individually as gallant as possible, have no collective confidence, to carry them on, nor officers to lead them.

The official view of the inadequacy of the Spanish troops was shared by everyone who had seen them. Baird's troops when passing through Astorga earlier on in the month had been horrified by the sight of half-starved men – some of whom were partly clothed in British uniforms and all of whom were strangely equipped and quite undisciplined – marching raggedly about 'in double-quick time with a wretched drum at the head of each regiment'.

Moore had now received a report that these troops, instead of marching from Leon to join him, were intending to retreat. 'I received upon my arrival yesterday afternoon', Moore wrote to the Marqués de la Romana on December 19th at Castro Nuevo,

> a letter from Sir David Baird, enclosing one which he had just received from you, dated the 16th; in which you mention your intention immediately to retreat, by Astorga and Villafranca into the Galicias. I beg to know whether this be still your Excellency's determination, as it is one which must materially affect my movements.... As it was my wish on coming here to combine my movements with those of the Spanish army under your command, I hope you will have the goodness to communicate to me your intentions.

Some pity could be felt for Romana who was so reluctant to bring into action his disgracefully treated army, so scantily clothed, so badly fed and

---

* The brigading of the various regiments is given in Appendix 1.

so crudely equipped; but nothing but angry contempt was felt for the leaders of the country and the people themselves who even in the best of times had not been friendly and were now openly hostile and shut their doors against the British troops and treated them like enemies. They were a nation not worth saving, Lord Paget told Holland in extravagant disdain, expressing a universal opinion of his Lordship's 'horrid protégés':

> Such ignorance, such deceit, such apathy, such pusillanimity, such cruelty was never before united. There is not one army that has fought at all. There is not one general who has exerted himself. There is not one province that has made any sacrifice whatever.... The resources of the country are withheld from us. We are roving about the country in search of Quixotic adventures to save our honour, whilst there is not a Spaniard who does not skulk and shrink within himself at the very name of Frenchman.

The sentiments were echoed in a letter written at Sahagun on the same day by Sir John Moore to Mr. Frere:

> If the British army were in an Enemy's country, it could not be more completely left to itself. If the Spaniards are enthusiasts, or much interested in their cause, their conduct is the most extraordinary that ever was exhibited.
>
> The movement I am making is of the most dangerous kind. I do not only risk to be surrounded every moment by superior forces, but to have my communications intercepted. I wish it to be apparent to the whole world, as it is to every individual of the army, that we have done everything in our power in support of the Spanish cause, and that we do not abandon it until long after the Spaniards had abandoned us.

The feelings were strongly put but they were not unjustified. Before the snow had covered the earth and the sky had turned a misty grey, a few towns and villages had welcomed the English soldiers. At Toro the plaza had been illuminated by flambeaux arranged on every balcony and 'windows were filled with ladies waving their handkerchiefs'; at Lombra the cannon on the ramparts roared and drums beat and trumpets sounded through the streets above the shouts of '*Viva los Ingleses!*' But these were isolated instances. The troops had become used to being received in a gloomy, suspicious silence. And now as they hurried through the thickly falling snow, past locked doors and through narrow empty streets, they began to conceive that hatred for the unseen Spaniards which was soon to reach its climax in violence and shame.

On December 21st, as the army moved on north-east to Sahagun beyond Astorga and Melgar Abaxo, the snow continued to fall. In the early morning the snowstorm ceased for a few hours and the grey sky was violently illuminated by several flashes of lightning. An Irish soldier looked up and crossed himself. He felt for a moment as if the army was marching in that soundless snow and beneath that angry sky to the very edge of the world.

In front of him Lord Paget was driving the French cavalry out of Sahagun. He had reached the outskirts of the town before dawn with the 10th and 15th Hussars and as the French had no outlying vedettes he had been able to surprise and capture five men of the main guard. The rest escaped, however, and galloped back into the town to give the alarm. The trumpets sounded shrilly in the streets as Paget ordered General Slade to take the 10th Hussars and charge in from the front, while he himself took the 15th Hussars round the town to cut off the retreat of the French on the far side. By the time the 15th Hussars had reached the rear of the village, however, General Slade had still not entered it from the front.

He was a slow and cautious man, and although he was forty-seven this was his first battle. He was determined to carry it through in the grand manner. He made elaborate dispositions, issued lengthy orders, laboriously satisfied himself that his troops were arranged to his design. Half a century later he still remembered it all with pride and described his careful plans to numerous dismayed great-grandchildren, to whom the charge of the Light Brigade at Balaclava was already a part of history. On this occasion, while Lord Paget, already on the far side of Sahagun with 400 hussars, found himself face to face with 600 French dragoons, John Slade was making the men of the 10th Hussars a long speech of encouragement which he concluded, so one of them reported, with the energetic and violent peroration: 'Blood and Slaughter – March!'

Lord Paget had decided that he could wait for Slade no longer. The French 8th Dragoons were extending in line with the 1st Provisional Chasseurs; and although the stumps and low stone walls of a vineyard, half concealed in the snow, were making it difficult for them to form, they would soon be ready. Paget looked over their heads but could see no sign of Slade.

The French were less than a quarter of a mile away across the expanse of untrodden snow and presented an imposing spectacle. The black horse-hair streamed from their brass helmets as they trotted into position on their strong horses, not one of which was less than fourteen-and-a-half hands. The 15th Hussars watched them in silence, their hands so benumbed in the intense cold that they could scarcely feel their reins or hold their swords. They looked in admiration at the gleaming helmets with the thick brass chains beneath the chin which gave protection against a horizontal *coup de sabre*. One officer felt deeply the inadequacy of his own fur cap, lined and stiffened with paste-board, which became heavy and soggy when wet, which fell off so easily in dry weather and guarded his skull not at all. The French fur caps, he knew, were lined with hoops of iron and strengthened with bars around the ears.

At last Paget gave his men the order to charge, and they galloped down the hill cheering and shouting 'Emsdorf and Victory!' The French dragoons only had time to fire a few shots from their carbines before the 15th had covered the 400 yards between them. The shock of impact, an officer said, 'was terrible; horses and men were overthrown and a shriek of terror, intermixed with oaths, groans, and prayers for mercy, issued from the whole extent of their front'. The frantic struggle continued for only a few minutes; then the French dragoons broke and fled. The 15th galloped after them having forgotten the cold in the excitement of the chase, slashing and jabbing at the enemy as they rushed across the vineyard, the snow flying from their horses' hooves. In the confusion Captain Gordon heard the crack of a pistol behind him and looked round to see one of his men fall. He thought the man was dead, until he was 'quickly undeceived by a burst of laugher from his comrades, who explained that the awkward fellow had shot his own horse'.

It was a decisive victory. Twenty French cavalrymen were killed, many more were wounded. There were 170 prisoners, including two colonels and eleven other officers. The strength of the *chasseurs,* commanded by Colonel Tascher, a cousin of the Empress Josephine, was so badly depleted that they had to be dissolved and replaced in General Franceski's division by the 1st Hussars. Sahagun was cleared of the enemy and later on that day General Moore entered it and made his Headquarters in a wing of the Benedictine convent which sprawled across half the town. That night he finished his preparations for an attack on Soult's positions beyond the Carrion, now less than twenty miles away. As soon as his stores caught up with him he intended to march his men through the night from Sahagun to Saldana and attack Soult at dawn. Since the cavalry engagement fought that morning there could be no doubt that Soult would be expecting him, but he would not know where or when. Before Moore went to bed in the early morning of December 22nd, a thick fog came down, enveloping the whole army in damp, impenetrable white and offering the hope of a surprise attack.

For the whole of that day, the troops rested and waited. The snow continued to fall and the fog lay heavy in the air. Every sound was muffled and even the wagons on their difficult journey from Mayorga, creaking through the streets with their loads of meat and biscuit, seemed to strike a softer, unfamiliar note. The men knew that the French were close at hand now and, looking across the white plain through the drifting fog, derived pleasure from the thought that they were going to have a fight at last. By New Year's Day, perhaps, their pockets would be full of loot and they would be drunk in Burgos.

The next day orders for the renewed advance were issued and in the evening the troops set out, cheering loudly as they left the town. The weather had become suddenly warmer during the afternoon, and the snows had melted. As the streets filled with slush, and the watery snow spattered from the roof tops, a heavy rain began to fall.

For hours Moore had been receiving messages from spies and officers that the French were marching from Madrid to Soult's assistance. He believed, however, that he would still have time to strike his blow before Napoleon could cross the Douro. If he could carry out his main attack on Christmas Day, he would still be able to turn and run back across the mountains to the sea before he was caught. But at six o'clock, as he sat astride his charger and Captain George Napier handed him his pistols, a Spanish peasant was brought to him with an urgent note from the Marqués de la Romana, who said that his agents on the Douro reported that all the French from Madrid were moving 'in this direction'. A little later one of Moore's own officers, sent down into the Castilian plain to give warning of any French movements in the south, confirmed that Romana's warning was justified. The French were much nearer than Moore, even in his most gloomy moments, had supposed. He realised at once that there was now no possible chance of defeating Soult before the French were upon him. By the time he had attacked Soult and returned to Sahagun, he would find an army of overwhelming force blocking his retreat. For the French were reported to be already far north of the Guadarramas; peasants had been ordered to collect large supplies of food and forage in villages west of Palencia; cavalry patrols had been seen less than a hundred miles away trotting along the banks of the Carrion. Napoleon himself was said to be close behind them.

The reports were true. On the evening of December 19th Napoleon was given information which indicated that the British army was not in retreat to Portugal but was advancing towards Burgos in Old Castile. He had been about to leave for the Portuguese frontier himself, but he cancelled his arrangements and held up the departure of 40,000 troops due to leave Madrid that week. He had three deserters from the 60th brought in to him and their answers to his questions persuaded him that at least a part of the English force was near the Carrion. He gave instructions for any other information which confirmed this supposition to be brought to him immediately. On the afternoon of December 21st, he was given more intelligence and made an immediate decision. He quickly ended a review of his troops and prepared to march in person against Moore, 'the only general', as he thought him, 'now worthy to contend with me'.

It meant giving up his other projects for the moment. To turn north instead of south would put back some time the conquest of Andalusia and the crossing of the Mediterranean. But the English must be destroyed. He must make an example of them and give a lesson to the world. Ney was ordered to forget Saragossa and advance from Aragon into Old Castile in support of Soult who was to drag Moore on to Burgos. He himself would cross the Sierra de Guadarrama with the Imperial Guard and attack the English in flank. 80,000 men would fall on them. By the morning of December 22nd, the cavalry of the Guard had already reached the Guadarrama pass. 'If only these 20,000 were 100,000,' Napoleon wrote in the excitement of anticipation, 'if only more English mothers could feel the horrors of war.' He was possessed by a passion for destruction and revenge. The day he saw these perfidious English would be 'a day of ecstasy'.

He arrived at Chamartin to find Lapisse's infantry had not yet crossed the mountains. The cavalry ahead of them had been caught in a blizzard and had stumbled back, almost blinded by the swirling snow and the biting, howling wind which had hurled several horses over the precipice. But, when the Emperor was reported close at hand, they had made another effort and this time struggled across to Villacastin leaving the path open for the infantry. It was still snowing hard as the infantry began their march. Three times the advance guard halted and said they could not go on in such conditions; but Napoleon would not be stopped. Men were sent forward to trample down the snow into a smooth track for the guns and the ammunition wagons; half the artillery carriages were unharnessed so that double teams could be given to the rest; pioneers were put to work to dig out the wheels of carts stuck in snow drifts. Napoleon himself pushed on with his escort through the struggling ranks, past exhausted soldiers, who shouted unheard curses at him into the whining wind. At the head of the column he dismounted, and surrounded by the officers of his staff he marched on, a small, huddled, silent, irresistible figure, to the top of the pass.

At seven o'clock in the evening of December 23rd he arrived at Villacastin and threw himself down on a sofa. He believed that Moore was less than seventy miles north of him at Valladolid and that he would soon be across his line of retreat at Medina de Rioseco.

Had Moore been at Valladolid, his army would have been destroyed. It was fortunate for him that Napoleon found it as difficult as he did to get accurate information of enemy movements and that he was fifty miles further north than his enemy supposed. If he retreated now from Sahagun, he might get back to Astorga and across the Esla before he was caught.

'It would only be losing the army to Spain and to England to persevere in my march on Soult', he wrote late that night to Romana. 'Single-handed I cannot pretend to contend with the superior numbers the French can now bring against me.' Romana was asked to take his men back across the Esla into the Asturias by the easiest and most northerly route which would leave the road to Astorga, and thence across the Cantabrian mountains into Galicia, clear for the British. Moore suggested that the Spaniards should cross the Esla at Mansilla, hold the bridge there as long as they could and thus give the British time to establish defensive positions in the mountains beyond Astorga without fear of being outflanked on their northern side. Within a few hours the British infantry would evacuate Sahagun. Baird's division would take the upper road to the Esla; Hope's and Fraser's divisions the lower one; the reserve division, the two light brigades and the cavalry would act as a rearguard to cover the withdrawal. 'If we can steal two marches on the French', he found time to write in his journal, 'we shall be quiet.' But he was well aware of the appalling difficulties and hardships of a fast retreat by corps in succession through a barren winter countryside without fuel and in which it was impossible to bivouac. The towns and villages on the way were small and widely separated; his inadequate commissariat would not be able to eke out its scanty supplies from the frozen, snow-covered wastes.

He was concerned too by the composition of the army. There were many women and children still with it; far too many criminals and Irishmen who fought well enough in battle but were neither easily controlled in adversity nor readily persuaded of the necessity for a withdrawal. Their reaction to the sudden change of plan was predictable. They listened to their officers' explanations with unconcealed disgust and an ominous rumble of protest. Outside the Benedictine convent Sir David Baird told the men of the 42nd Royal Highland Regiment to hold themselves ready for a retreat at dawn. When he had spoken, the Highlanders stood for several moments, 'transfixed', one of their officers, a young boy of sixteen, wrote afterwards.

> And at length their disappointment broke out into a murmur....Indeed the effect of this counter-order on our soldiers was the most extraordinary; and from the greatest pitch of exaltation and courage at once a solemn gloom prevailed throughout our ranks. Nothing was heard on every side but the clang of firelocks thrown down in despair, which before they guarded as their dearest treasure.

They returned to their quarters, Charles Stewart said, 'in a state of sullen silence'.

Rifleman Harris, a young cobbler with the 95th, already several miles north of Sahagun on the road to Carrion, was marching along quite cheerfully under a full moon, when at about two o'clock in the morning he 'observed a dragoon come spurring furiously' up the road to deliver a letter to Colonel Craufurd at the head of the column. Craufurd read a few lines, then turned round in his saddle and thundered out the command 'Halt!' A few minutes later the whole of Craufurd's Light Brigade had turned about and were retracing their steps of the previous night. It was light by the time they reached Sahagun again. It had been freezing for the last few hours and the roads, 'dreadfully cut up by the guns', were so rutted and icy that the men could scarcely keep on their feet. In the village square their shoes slithered on the slippery cobbles as their wives and children rushed out to meet them, to push into the ranks to kiss and hug them, not caring that they were exhausted, sullen and retreating, happy that at least they were still alive.

PART THREE

The Retreat

6

Sahagun to Astorga

'The people run away, the villages are deserted, and I have been obliged to destroy great part of the ammunition and military stores. For the same reason I am obliged to leave the sick. In short, my sole object is to save the Army.'

Sir John Moore

IT WAS CHRISTMAS EVE and it was raining. Hope's and Fraser's divisions had left for Astorga; the rest of the army were due to leave for the Esla on Christmas Day. The men waited in the gloomy little town of Sahagun in a mood of savage ill-temper. 'Each spoke to his fellow,' a soldier in the 71st said, 'even in common conversation, with bitterness; rage flashing in their eyes, even on the most trifling occasions of disagreement.' In the vineyards to the east of the town, the bodies of the French dragoons lay in the slush. Stripped by peasants and the boys of the town, the corpses lay bedraggled and half-naked where they had fallen. Before the ground had been too hard to bury them; now they were left, with dogs roving around them and birds pecking at their eyes, to await burial by their comrades who would soon be back.

For three days it went on raining. The troops marched back on roads and tracks which in the morning were covered in frost and ice and by noon were ankle-deep in mud. Their behaviour was appalling. Almost every village through which they passed, a cavalry officer of the rearguard reported,

exhibited melancholy proofs of the shameful devastation committed by the infantry which had preceded us; we observed one in flames whilst we were at a considerable distance, and it was still burning when we passed through it. The inhabitants shouted 'Viva los Francesces!' and we overtook some stragglers who had been stripped and maltreated by the Spaniards.

As a sign of their relief and, as Quartermaster-Sergeant Surtees of the 95th put it, 'to evince their gratitude to Heaven for having got rid of such a band of heretics', the villagers rang their church bells as soon as the last English soldier had gone.

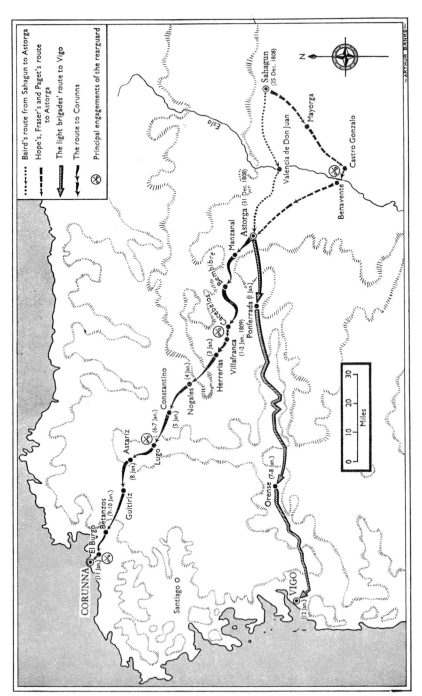

The retreat of the British Forces from Sahagun to Vigo and Corunna

Legend:

········ Baird's route from Sahagun to Astorga
━ ━ ━ Hope's, Fraser's and Paget's route to Astorga
▨▨▨ The light brigades' route to Vigo
↓ The route to Corunna
⊗ Principal engagements of the rearguard

—ARTHUR BANKS—

The officers were quite unable to control their men whose passion for drink and for loot was ungovernable. On one occasion Colonel Eley, a tall and powerful officer, was seen giving a German hussar 'a most unmerciful thrashing with the flat of his sword' because he refused to relinquish some loot he had discovered and rejoin his regiment. The hussar dodged from side to side, doing his best to ward off the blows but clinging fast to his prize.

Despite their indiscipline, however, most of the men moved fast for there was little worth risking a flogging for in that waste of mud; and on December 26th Baird's division reached the Esla. They found it a swirling torrent of still rising water. The ford at Valencia de Don Juan was not yet in flood, however, and they crossed over in safety. On the far side though, some of the men sank up to their cross-belts in the liquid mud which filled the deeply rutted track.

As yet they had seen no sign of the enemy, for on Christmas Day Napoleon had rested his army at Tordesillas, fifty miles to the south. But, on the road behind Baird's retreating infantry, Soult's cavalry had caught up with the cavalry of the rearguard and were tentatively feeling their strength. Lord Paget was determined to make them believe it was greater than it was. Every prod was parried; each exploratory attack was met by a counter-charge; whenever there was an opening he took full advantage of it to become the aggressor and not the pursued. He was, as one of his officers justly said, 'magnificent and tireless', and so were his men.

General Slade, however, the commander of his second brigade, was neither; and Lord Paget despised him for it. Years afterwards, as a hero of Waterloo and the first Marquess of Anglesey, acknowledged as Europe's most brilliant cavalry leader, Paget still felt for Slade, despite Wellington's more favourable judgment, a deep and angry rancour. 'The fellow was a bungler', he said of him and the tone of his voice indicated that Slade was not merely that. Even at the time he was so exasperated by what he took to be the man's complete stupidity that he went so far as to make his contempt quite obvious to both officers and men. On one occasion he gave some orders to Slade regarding the order of march and the precautions to be adopted when executing it. No sooner had Slade ridden away than Lord Paget called one of his aides-de-camp and in an inexcusably loud voice told him to 'ride after that damned stupid fellow' to see that he made no mistake.

In his first important action of the retreat, Slade behaved as he had done a few days before at Sahagun. He was directed by Paget to attack the enemy's approaching cavalry with a squadron of the 10th Hussars. Slade moved off at a trot but had only gone a few yards when he halted to have some alteration made in the length of his stirrups. His men were halted too while the alteration was made. At length his stirrups were comfortable; and again the squadron advanced, but again before the General had gone far, he halted his men once more while he had an orderly readjust his straps. Lord Paget watched him in growing irritation and then, unable any longer to bear the sight of the orderly fiddling with the bungler's stirrups, he rode up and told Colonel Leigh to take over. With Leigh at their head, the 10th charged gallantly, broke through the lines of horsemen and, slashing many from their saddles, with little loss on their part galloped off with forty prisoners. It was an inspiring sight.

Each of Lord Paget's regiments performed in the next fortnight a feat of similar dash. On the day after the 10th's attack, the 18th Light Dragoons turned round on their pursuers six times and each time charged them so successfully that they were left in peace for the next few miles. Once, as the infantry were crossing the Esla at Valencia de Don Juan, thirty-eight dragoons charged over a hundred of the enemy and breaking through killed twelve of them and captured twenty. But, although Napoleon was to put their numbers at between 4,000 and 5,000 the numbers of the cavalry were less than 2,400; and it was impossible for them to prevent infiltrations by a cavalry force which was more than three times as strong. Baird's division had reached the Esla without mishap, but Hope's and Fraser's divisions on the more southerly road to the bridge at Castro Gonzalo were harried by squadrons of light cavalry, which had slipped through Lord Paget's extended screen.

As Baird's men stumbled in the driving rain up the mud-covered tracks beyond Valencia de Don Juan, the other two divisions crossed the bridge at Castro Gonzalo. Two sharp-sighted men, private soldiers of the 43rd, John Walton and Richard Jackson, were posted on high ground near the bridge with orders that on the approach of the enemy one man should stand firing while the other ran back to give warning of their numbers. It was difficult to see clearly through the torrential rain and the French cavalry were close upon them and had already captured some women and baggage carts before the two men saw their danger. Jackson stood up and ran for all he was worth to give the alarm, turning to fire when he heard the galloping hooves behind him. He received twelve or fourteen cuts from the slashing sabres of the French hussars; but he crawled away and escaped to warn his regiment while Walton stood his ground, firing his musket while he could and lunging with his bayonet when the riders were on top of him. He wounded several of them and the rest retired, leaving him unhurt although his knapsack, belt and musket were cut in about twenty places and his bayonet, dripping blood into the churned-up earth at his feet, was bent double and notched like a saw.

During the late afternoon of December 28th the last straggler from

Hope's division passed through the village of Castro Gonzalo and crossed the stone bridge. The light had almost gone and the rain still poured down from a slate-coloured sky. The men of Robert Craufurd's light brigade, with the water running out of the muzzles of their rifles, were drawn up in a semicircular line in the mud on the eastern side of the bridge to act as a rearguard while the cavalry splashed past them. 'Whilst we stood thus,' a rifleman of the 95th wrote,

> I remember the horsemen of the enemy sat watching us very intently, as if waiting for a favourable moment to dash upon us like beasts of prey; and every now and then their trumpets would ring out with a lively strain of music, as if to encourage them.... General Craufurd was wrapped in his greatcoat, and, like ourselves, had been for many hours drenched to the skin, for the rain was coming down furiously. He carried in his hand a canteen full of rum, and a small cup, with which he was occasionally endeavouring to refresh some of the men. He offered me a drink as he passed and then proceeded onwards along the bridge. After he had emptied his canteen, he came past us again, and himself gave us instructions as to our future proceedings.
>
> 'When all is ready, Riflemen,' said he, 'you will immediately get the word and pass over the bridge. Be careful, and mind what you are about!'

As they watched the enemy, the engineers behind them were preparing to blow up the bridge. They had been working for many hours now, but the masonry was so solid that they doubted that they would get their charges deep enough in the stonework before the French galloped over the bridge in force and threw them off it. During the night three squadrons of *chasseurs* charged the light brigade pickets and were repelled, but later on some of them dismounted and tried to break through on foot. The light brigade held its ground, however, and the work of demolition continued.

All the next day, while the infantry columns entered Benavente, the engineers worked on the bridge and Craufurd's men held back the threat of the French cavalry whose scouts could be seen trotting undisturbed all over the plain. At midnight the charges were in position at last and the order to blow the bridge was given. The powder was packed so deep that the noise of detonation was no more than a rumbling boom above the roar of the rising river and for an agonised second the waiting, listening men feared that their work had all been in vain. But then the thick stone split and two arches with their connecting buttress tumbled down into the swollen waters of the Esla. Hidden from the French scouts in the darkness of the night the men of the rearguard crossed over to the other bank, walking in single file on planks laid across the broken arches, keeping their eyes on the cross belts of the men in front, making no sound above the roar of the rushing river and the bluster of the wind. One of them, worn out by the exertions of the past few days, thought that if he ever managed to control his trembling legs long enough to reach the other end of the plank, that would be as far as he would ever get. 'I was now so utterly helpless', he wrote, 'that I felt as if all was nearly up with me. However, we managed all of us to reach the other side in safety.'

When the last man was across, the engineers lit their final charges and blew the central arch of the bridge into the river with such force that Rifleman Harris was thrown flat upon his face to the ground, 'almost in a state of insensibility'. 'After a while I recovered,' he said, 'but it was not without extreme difficulty, and many times falling again, that I succeeded in regaining the columns. Soon after I had done so, we reached Benavente, and immediately took refuge in a convent.'

The engineers had done their work at Castro Gonzalo so well that the French took twenty-four hours to repair the bridge. They need not have been so thorough, however, for the enterprising Quartermaster-Sergeant Surtees of the 95th, determined to keep his men well supplied with biscuit during the remainder of the retreat, took a cart and two bullocks, loaded with an immense quantity of biscuit he had found stored in an empty house in the village, straight into the river at a place that looked like a ford. He drove them blindly on and using his sword as a goad managed to reach the other side and bring his load into the town of Benavente, where Moore had taken advantage of the destruction of the bridge and the supposed flooding of the fords, to give his exhausted men a day's rest and an opportunity to reorganise.

Discipline was breaking fast and the General doubted that the army could survive an attack in its present mood and condition. He had been deeply shocked by the appalling behaviour of the troops who had shown themselves capable of any crime in their lust for alcohol. Their habit of tearing the buttons from their coats and passing them off on the Spanish as English coin and their trick of stealing wine in borrowed uniforms so that they could not afterwards be recognised, were their least offences. They were capable sometimes of murder and frequently of violence.

When the 52nd entered its quarters in the monastery on the outskirts of Benevente, the 'holy fat father abbot declared', so Ensign Robert Blakeney said, 'by a long catalogue of saints that there was not a drop' of wine to be had. A sergeant found a newly built wall in an outhouse, however, and felt sure that behind it the friars had concealed their vats. An officer had himself lowered on a rope into the outhouse through a skylight and two men of his company followed him. They found, as they had suspected, an enormous vat filled with wine.

And, while they were issuing it out in perfect order to the drenched and shivering soldiers, the fat prior suddenly made his appearance through a trap-door, and laughingly requested that at least he might have one drink before all was consumed. Upon this one of the men remarked 'By Jove! When the wine was his, he was damned stingy about it; but now that it is ours, we will show him what British hospitality is, and give him his fill.' So saying, he seized the holy fat man, and chucked him head foremost into the vat.

Following the example of the 52nd, other regiments as soon as they entered the town went in search of wine and nothing that the officers could say or do or threaten prevented them from wandering off at random. Many officers, indeed, accepting the impossibility of control, left their men to roam the streets at will. Soon, in an extensive range of vaults beneath a square, hundreds of pipes of wine were found and rolled up the steps on to the paving stones. At sight of the casks the soldiers fired their muskets at them, but instead of puncturing holes in the top as they expected the balls broke them up altogether and the wine gushed out in all directions until the streets were ankle-deep in it. The men sank to their knees and drank it like water.

From his Headquarters in the town Moore observed the disintegration of the weaker regiments and the incapacity of some of their officers and wrote a General Order of unusual asperity:

> The Commander of the Forces has observed with concern the extreme bad conduct of the troops at a moment when they are about to come into contact with the Enemy, and when the greatest regularity and the best conduct are the most requisite.... The misbehaviour of the troops in the column which marched by Valderas to this place, exceeds what he could have believed of British soldiers. It is disgraceful to the Officers; as it strongly marks their negligence and inattention....
>
> It is impossible for the General to explain to his army the motive for the movement he directs. The Commander of the Forces can, however, assure the army that he has made none since he left Salamanca which he did not foresee, and was not judged prepared for; and, as far as he is a judge, they have answered the purposes for which they were intended.
>
> When it is proper to fight a battle he will do it; and he will choose the time and place he thinks fit: in the meantime he begs the Officers and Soldiers of the army to attend diligently to discharge their parts and to leave to him and to the General Officers the decision of measures which belong to them alone....

The Order was merited; but the misbehaviour and bad conduct of which he complained were as yet inconsiderable compared with what was later to take place. That evening, in the large convent at Benavente and in the castle of the Duchess of Ossuna nearby, the troops behaved in the outrageous way which was to characterise the retreat. In the convent, shutters and doors were torn loose from the walls and tables and benches were smashed to feed the fires which burned fiercely in every room. Casks of sacramental wine were broken open and, when the contents had been drunk, the casks were thrown on to the flames. In the lower corridors, where horses were packed like eels in a barrel, a shutter caught fire and the flames had already spread to the rafters before the danger was noticed. Sparks were dropping on to the backs of the horses and would soon have ignited the straw beneath their legs, had not Captain Lloyd of the 43rd Regiment jumped up on to the back of the nearest horse and, running along the backs of the others down the narrow corridor until he came to the burning shutter, wrenched it from its hinges and thrown it into the courtyard.

Fires also broke out that night in the Duchess of Ossuna's castle which the soldiers had almost gutted in their reckless search for fuel and drink. It was a crumbling building of a strange and haunting beauty, with tall turrets richly ornamented by fretwork as delicate as filigree and towers whose summits were bound round with massive chains of sculptured stone. 'A castle surpassing anything I had ever seen', a soldier of the 31st thought it. 'It was such, on our arrival, as I have read the descriptions of in books of fairy tales.'

The Duchess had fled to Seville with her daughters and her *cortego* to escape from the French, so the castle was empty. She returned to find it ravaged and desolate. Whole floors had been ripped out; gilt furniture of great age and matchless beauty was splintered or in ashes; the panelling and beautifully carved columns bore the scratches and incisions of hundreds of bayonets; the seventeenth-century tapestries lay ripped and crumpled where the soldiers had thrown them down after using them as blankets. Outside in the courtyard, where soldiers' wives had lit great fires to boil their camp kettles and wash their clothes, the once white walls were scorched and blackened. Everywhere there were broken casks, heaps of broken biscuit and rotting meat, kettles full of sour wine. For Benavente had been an advanced stores depot and the Commissariat had offered the men anything they needed and could carry away with them. There was no time for a fair distribution or organisation to cope with one. Piles of clothing and food were heaped up on the road leading out of Benavente to the north, and when the troops left on the morning of December 29th they were told to help themselves to as much as they could carry.

On the outskirts of the town, in the garden of the monastery which had been used as a warehouse, thousands of pairs of shoes, wagonloads of biscuit, salted meat, shirts, blankets, stockings and belts were thrown into great heaps by raging bonfires; while the townspeople, drawn by the noise and the smoke, ran up to accept the Englishmen's offer to take what they could before everything was thrown to the flames, and to scoop up from the gutters the gallons of rum which poured from the staved-in casks. Then amid shouts of '*Viva! Viva los Ingleses!*' from grateful Spaniards, who had suddenly become the owners of more food and clothing than they had ever owned at one time before, the officers of the Commissariat jumped astride their horses and galloped away after the retreating infantry.

The infantry of the rearguard had left the town and Major Colborne was packing up his papers and preparing to rejoin the General and the rest of the staff on the road to La Bañeza, when a dragoon with a naked sabre galloped past his tent flap. Colborne's servant hurried out to ask what was the matter and ran back to say to his master, 'The French are crossing the river, sir'.

'Well, make haste', said Colborne, not for a moment considering the possibility of catching up with the staff while there was a battle to see. 'Make haste. Take on my baggage as fast as you can.' And he dashed back to the Esla.

The bridge had not yet been properly repaired but several horses had managed to cross by the ford a few hundred yards downstream where Sergeant Surtees had got over with his wagon-load of biscuit the night before. 'It was an immense plain', Colborne wrote later. 'The French were crossing the river, and our cavalry waiting to receive them. Lord Paget, who commanded, galloped up twirling his moustachios, and said "You see, there are not many of them".' By the time they had all crossed, however, there were between five and six hundred of them. They were *chasseurs* of the Imperial Guard, commanded by General Lefebvre-Desnouettes, and they presented an imposing and unnerving sight. Having formed up in line, they came on slowly but confidently, pushing back the pickets of the 18th Light Dragoons.

Lord Paget's early calm seemed scarcely justified. General Slade's brigade was slow to form and, for his first counter-charge, Colonel Otway had the support of only 130 men. The counter-charge was held and repulsed and the *chasseurs* came on again. As Otway rallied and reformed his men on higher ground, however, he was joined by Major Burgwedel with a troop of the King's German Legion. Thus reinforced he charged again, and this time the British and German dragoons together broke through the first line of the *chasseurs*. But their numbers were insufficient to maintain the fight and again they withdrew, and were taken back by Charles Stewart to the suburbs of Benavente, where Lord Paget had now managed to form up the 10th Hussars behind a fold of the ground which concealed them from the view of the advancing *chasseurs*.

Paget waited until the French had come more than two miles from the river line and then, with 450 men of the 10th Hussars and 200 men from the 18th Light Dragoons and the King's German Legion, he appeared from his hiding-place and charged. For a few moments, as at Sahagun, there was a fierce struggle as the two lines crashed head on. Sabres flashed in the air and men fell tumbling to the ground at the feet of their blood-spattered horses. The heavy British swords, usually blunted by their metal scabbards, were on this occasion exquisitely sharp. Major Jesse of the King's German Legion saw several French arms sliced off, clean and neat, like Berlin sausages. He saw one Frenchman fall to the ground with the whole of the top of his head cut off horizontally above the eyes at one blow, and many others with their heads divided down to the chin.

When the *chasseurs* turned and galloped back to the river, they left fifty-five men dead or wounded on the field; and the British cavalry rode over their bodies as they chased the survivors to the ford. Behind them the people of Benavente rushed out of the town to cheer them on, excitedly shouting '*Viva los Ingleses!*' above the screams of the wounded and the thunder of galloping hooves. Most of the *chasseurs* managed to scramble and splash through the ford, but many did not escape. One of these rode into the river some distance from the ford but the water was too deep and the current too strong. He had to turn back and was captured by a trooper of the King's German Legion. But, before the German realised the value of his prize, a man of the 10th Hussars came and led the prisoner off and was promoted sergeant for having done so. For the dejected captive was General Comte Charles Lefebvre-Desnouettes himself.

Lefebvre-Desnouettes trotted sadly into Benavente, the blood pouring from a wound in his forehead, while the shots from a battery of horse artillery whistled over his head and into the broken ranks of his men falling back beyond the river.

At Headquarters later that day he was brought in to General Moore who noticed the wound on his forehead and asked for water so that he could wash it. When he had wiped the blood away Moore said it was only a superficial wound and would soon heal. He was more concerned by the Frenchman's wet clothes and offered him some of his own dry linen. Lefebvre-Desnouettes accepted the offer graciously but asked if he might send across the river for his own things. Moore agreed and sent a flag of truce to Castro Gonzalo to make the request. Within the hour a vast quantity of luggage was brought to Headquarters and Lefebvre-Des-nouettes appeared for dinner in a magnificent uniform, but without a sword. Moore asked him if he now had everything he wanted, and Lefebvre-Desnouettes glanced down at his side without speaking. Moore immediately unbuckled his own sword, a fine East Indian sabre, and handed it to him.

Before going in to dine, Moore quietly asked his Military Secretary if he thought it would be right to ask Lefebvre-Desnouettes for a written promise not to escape. Colborne advised not, as he 'remembered a French officer in Sicily being much affronted at such a request'. Sir John Moore said, 'I am glad you told me this. Of course, I will not ask.' As if to make up for having thought of making so embarrassing a request, Moore behaved with particular politeness towards the French General throughout the meal. But the unwilling guest remained in a despondent mood. The British staff had heard a rumour that Napoleon himself had watched the cavalry engagement from beyond the river; and Lefebvre-Desnouettes commented gloomily that the Emperor never forgave the unfortunate.

The Emperor, for the moment, however, had more important matters on his mind than the capture of an expendable general. From Tordesillas he had written hopefully to Soult, 'Our cavalry scouts are already at Benavente. If the English pass to-day in their positions they are lost.' He had hurried on himself towards the Esla, dragging his infantry with him, not yet sure exactly where the English army was, but confident that he would soon find out and destroy it. 'Today or to-morrow', he wrote to his brother Joseph in Madrid on December 27th,

> it is probable that great events will take place. If the English have not already retreated they are lost. Even if they have already moved they shall be chased to the water's edge and not half of them shall re-embark. Put into your newspapers that 36,000 English are surrounded, that I am at Benavente in their rear while Soult is in their front.

Two days later he realised that, quick as he had been, he had not been quick enough. Moore had escaped. When the French reached the Esla, the English infantry were already leaving Benavente on the next stage of their march to Astorga.

But Napoleon still hoped that he might catch the English before they reached the mountain defiles beyond Astorga. If he crossed the river with the men he had brought with him from Madrid, and dashed west across the Leon plain while Soult crossed further upstream and came to join him from the north, he would have the English caught in that eagle's claw so dear to his heart. On December 29th while Lefebvre-Desnouettes rode along towards Astorga, guarded by riflemen of the 95th, one of whom noticed how 'chap-fallen and dejected' he looked, Napoleon's troops were already on the road to the bridge at Castro Gonzalo only fifteen miles behind.

On that same day Soult closed in on the bridge at Mansilla. The road from Sahagun was an appalling one and it had taken him three days to cover forty-five miles. Had he been able to move more quickly he might have destroyed Romana's crumbling army on the Leon plain east of the Esla, but as it was when he came up to Mansilla the bulk of the army had already crossed and only 3,000 men and two guns had been left to protect the bridge. Although they were men of Romana's 2nd Division, and perhaps the best of his troops, they were already broken in spirit when Franceski's dragoons and chasseurs charged into their lines on December 30th. Shivering with cold and hunger, they were helpless to resist so determined an attack and were herded back to the river like frightened cattle. More than half of them and both their guns were captured, and Soult's men poured across the river towards Leon, which they occupied the following day. Romana, asked by Moore to retreat across the Cantabrian mountains into the Asturias, reported that the pass at Pajares was blocked by snow; and so the Spaniards fell back towards the Astorga road to clog the already congested line of the British retreat.

While the Spanish army fell back headlong before Soult, the British retreated at an even faster pace before Napoleon.

'By Jasus! Mr. Hills,' Rifleman Harris heard an Irishman in his company ask their officer with breathless exasperation, 'where the devil is this you're taking us to?'

'To England, McLachlan,' replied the officer, with a melancholy smile upon his face, as he gave the answer ' – if we can get there.'

At every halt the same sort of questions were asked. Why were they running so fast? Why couldn't they turn round and fight? What did it matter if they got killed for the march was killing them anyway? Despite Moore's General Order issued at Benavente many officers joined in these angry discussions. The General was very much blamed, one of them said afterwards, for his absolute silence regarding the reasons for his movement. 'It was the wrong time for secrecy and he ought to have acquainted all officers and men with the necessity for the retreat long before.'

Soon regiments with a high proportion of criminals had become openly mutinous. Officers were not merely disobeyed but insulted. Stragglers could be seen stretching for miles over the flat plains and even the reports that the French were close behind, and would kill them rather than be troubled with prisoners, did not persuade them to close up to the main columns. It had become colder and the snow was falling again and the mules and bullocks, like the stragglers, could not keep up the pace and fell down to die by the roadside. And as the animals collapsed the soldiers' wives lifted down their children from the top of the stores and baggage in the carts and continued on foot.

On the last day of 1808 the infantry of the rearguard stumbled into Astorga.

The town was crammed with troops. Every large house, every convent, every church was a barracks or a storehouse; and the buildings not occupied by British troops contained the remnants of Romana's army. The Spanish soldiers had been without food for several days; many of them were barefoot; many more had lost their muskets or thrown them away after firing off the remains of their ammunition to keep their hands warm. Their clothes were in rags. Most of them had typhus fever; some of them were dying and some of them were dead. The British stole their artillery mules and the Spanish officers with strength enough to protest were told to 'mind their own bloody business'. Insult bred insult; outrage bred outrage; Spaniards and British alike roamed the streets like bandits and soon no house in Astorga was safe from either.

As at Benavente, so here, the men soon found and broke open the heavy, tombstone-like doors of the *bodegas,* and as the wine cascaded into the streets mixing with army rum from staved-in casks, they took off their caps and scooping it up in them 'drank, or rather ate the swinish mixture'. Real food, however, was not so easily found, for the stores in Astorga contained only two days' supply. Jaded cart bullocks were shot down and hastily carved up, cooked and eaten in the streets; but these were not enough to feed an army which with the Spaniards still numbered more than 30,000 men. The nearest large supply of food was at Villafranca, fifty miles further back in the west, and Moore felt that he had no alternative but to get there.

The former plan, still advocated by Romana, of defending the mountain passes behind Astorga had to be abandoned. 'There is no means of carriage', Moore had written home to Lord Castlereagh in an explanatory despatch on New Year's Eve. 'The people run away, the villages are deserted; and I have been obliged to destroy great part of the ammunition and military stores. For the same reason I am obliged to leave the sick. In short, my sole object is to save the Army.' He could not save it at Astorga. Draught animals were dying in hundreds; their drivers were deserting; the Commissariat, with these difficulties added to their normal ones, was collapsing. Thousands of blankets and shoes had been brought out of the stores, but the incompetent officials had burned half of them before either the Spanish or the British army was fully equipped. There was the danger too that, if he made a stand at Astorga, the French might get behind him, either on the north side by pushing through from Leon towards Villafranca or on his south by means of mountain tracks between Benavente and Orense. He must, he felt convinced, get back to Villafranca and then, perhaps, in the passes of the Cantabrian mountains beyond the town he would feel more secure. The sea at Corunna or Vigo would not be much more than a hundred miles behind him there, and if he were defeated he would have a reasonable chance of reaching it. To be defeated at Astorga would be to lose an army, already half way to perdition.

And so in the last few hours of 1808 the rearguard of the army left Astorga: the two light brigades under Robert Craufurd and Karl Alten on the road for Orense and Vigo; the Reserve and the 15th Hussars on the road to Bembibre and Villafranca, which the rest of the army had already taken. The other cavalry regiments had also gone ahead as they could be of little further use in the constricting mountains that lay ahead. Both Lord Paget and Charles Stewart were suffering from ophthalmia, so the 15th Hussars were, to Edward Paget's disgust, put under command of John Slade.

The roads led steeply up into the mountains and they were covered with ice. There was no moon. The troops cursed as they slipped and struggled up the defiles. And then they fell into silence. In the early hours of the morning Lieutentant Hill of the 95th said to a fellow officer, 'This is New Year's Day! I think if we live we shall not easily forget it.' Soon afterwards the officer to whom he spoke sank down into the snow and died.

7

Astorga to Villafranca

'My God! Is it not lamentable to think that, instead of preparing the troops
confided to my command to receive the enemies of their country, I am
preparing to hang two robbers?'

> Major-General the Hon. Edward Paget

'THE ENGLISH are running away as fast as they can', Napoleon wrote from
Benavente, giving instructions for vivid descriptions of their disgusting
behaviour to be put in the newspapers. 'They have abandoned the
Spaniards in a shameful and cowardly manner.' Caricatures were to be
drawn, songs and pamphlets written and translated into German and
Italian; accounts of their drunkenness and violence and their habit of
chasing nuns were to be widely circulated. Regard for accuracy was not
to be allowed to interfere with the imagination of the writers who were,
for example, told to describe the British sacking of Leon although their
army had not passed within thirty miles of it. It must be clearly shown,
Napoleon said in another context, that 'all the evils, all the plagues which
can afflict the human race, come from London'.

He himself would not bother with them any longer. Reducing the size
of the British army from 36,000 to '21,000 infantry with 4,000 or 5,000
horses', he decided to leave their destruction to Marshal Soult as soon as
he heard that they had reached the mountains. In one of those theatrical
scenes which gave to his most calculated actions an air of dramatic urgency
and spontaneous decision, he paced up and down in front of his troops
while they were halted on the road to Astorga, holding in his hand a
despatch which a courier from Paris had just given him. There were
stories of plots in France, revolutionaries in Turkey, unrest in Austria.
His Empire could manage without his dynamic presence no longer. He
remounted his horse and galloped down the road as if he had that moment
arrived at a decision of supreme importance. Within days he was back in
Paris.

The Imperial Guard was ordered to go back to Valladolid; Debelle's
division to Madrid; Bonnet's division to garrison duties in Santander.
Lapisse's division was sent south to the Douro where Spanish patriots,

assisted by British agents, had turned out the French garrisons in Toro and Zamora and were preparing to withstand a siege. Junot's corps was reformed; some battalions being sent back to their headquarters, others being transferred to Soult's command, while Junot himself was sent to take a command under Lannes at the siege of Saragossa. This reorganisation gave Soult's 2nd Corps 25,000 infantry and 6,000 cavalry with 16,000 additional men under Ney in support. To push into the sea a British army, wasted by sickness and straggling to less than 25,000 men, these numbers seemed more than enough.

Throughout the night the rearguard had struggled against the wind and the driving snow along the winding track up Monte Toleno and through the great serpentine pass at the summit. All the way through it, a Highlander remembered 'the silence was only interrupted by the groans of the men who, unable to proceed farther, laid themselves down in despair to perish in the snow or when the report of a pistol told the death of a horse, which had fallen down, unable to proceed'.

Daylight brought no comfort. The mountain road turned and twisted so much between the sharp, overhanging peaks that the men seemed to make no headway. As far as they could see, the long ragged line of the army curled in and out, up and down, through the white wastes of snow, past abandoned carts and dead animals, over rushing mountain streams on bridges supported by immense boulders covered with ice. During the morning the wind fell and the snow turned to sleet and then to heavy rain, and the road became like a lake, on the still hard bed of which the men and horses walked up to their knees in watery mud. Sometimes they passed a group of huts or a mountain village where brown-skinned men with Moorish faces and strange gypsy clothing looked through the doorways of their windowless hovels, silently watching the terrible cavalcade. A German officer looked into one of these hovels and described the scene he found there:

> The fireplace was in the middle and the smoke went whither it listed, up to the roof or out at the door. The fuel consisted of moist heath; they do not burn any light throughout the long winter nights; but illumine their huts with their heath fires, the smoke of which makes the eyes smart horribly. The family in this particular hut consisted of a tall old black and yellow witch with three ugly children, of whom two were suffering from a hectic fever. Everything was extremely dirty; their hair was matted together, and they seemed never to have washed since the day of their birth. Round the woman's neck hung a rosary in three strands, ornamented with sacred medals, and she wore two huge earrings. She did nothing

except sit over the fire and shake with cold and misery. The whole place presented a picture of the most appalling wretchedness.

Other huts were full of corpse-like stragglers from Romana's army, begging helplessly for food or howling like dogs with the maddening ache of hunger. They screamed curses at their more fortunate fellow countrymen who crouched down in coaches, wagons, calashes and litters as their servants and animals dragged and carried them away from the approaching French towards Bembibre and then beyond to the safety of the coast.

Towards the end of New Year's Day the rearguard reached the tumbledown town of Bembibre, 'a wretched, filthy little hole' of small crumbling houses where the wine of the upland plateau was stored in vaults beneath the streets. They found every door and window broken, every lock forced. Hope's, Baird's and Fraser's divisions had passed through it like a horde of brigands and more than a thousand men were left behind in the streets too drunk to move. They lay in contorted, huddled groups and even the women and children had wine oozing from their lips and nostrils as if they had been shot. The men of the rearguard slapped their faces, prodded them with their bayonets and kicked them savagely; but most of them could not move, and although the 95th spent most of the day, as one of their sergeants said, 'in turning or dragging the drunken stragglers out of the houses into the streets and sending as many forward as could be moved . . . yet little could be effected with men incapable of standing much less of marching forward'. Eventually in a kind of piteous anger the officers of the reserve division told their men to give up and leave them.

A few hours later the last hussar pickets of the rearguard fell back through the town, shouting that a regiment of French dragoons was approaching the eastern gate. Soldiers and Spanish muleteers stumbled out of the vaults and lifted themselves up from the still prostrate bodies of women and tried to get away; but they had left it too late. Lahoussaye's dragoons came galloping after them, splashing through the puddles of mud and wine, slashing at the backs below them, killing or wounding everyone in their path. Only a few survivors, many of them appallingly mangled, managed to escape and rejoin the army on the road to Villafranca.

One of them caught up with a man on patrol from the 15th Hussars. Hearing a rustling amidst some stunted trees beside the road, the hussar looked round and caught sight of what he took to be a wild hog. He went closer and saw that it was a human figure creeping along with a blood-stained shirt drawn over the head to keep the frosty air from his fearful wounds. An officer of the regiment who later saw the hideously wounded man said he was

> the most shocking spectacle I ever beheld. It was impossible to distinguish a single feature. The flesh of his cheeks and lips was hanging in collops, his nose was split, and his ears, I think, were cut off. In addition to his wounds, it is probable that his limbs were frost-bitten, for it was quite horrible to see the manner in which he cowered near the fire, and raked the glowing embers towards him with his fingers.

Determined to give the men a warning which they would not easily forget, Moore gave orders that stragglers butchered in this way should be paraded past regiments drawn up specifically to see them. And in Villafranca, which the leading divisions reached on January 1st, the public exhibition of these piteous exhibits continued. But more than this was needed now to bring the army to its senses. For discipline, except in the rearguard and a few of the more orderly regiments such as the Guards, no longer existed. Officers had been forced to give up all attempts at control.

Villafranca, about twenty miles west of Bembibre, stands at the foot of the Cantabrian mountain range and here Moore had hoped, as at Astorga, that he might have been able to make a stand. The passes behind the town were ideal for defence and the stores in Villafranca were well stocked. Any hopes, however, he may still have had after seeing the behaviour of the troops at Bembibre were gone by the night of January 2nd. For during the previous day a riot had broken out in the town which did not end until after midnight. Houses and shops were plundered, churches pillaged, wine casks smashed open in the streets. The commissaries were pushed aside in the stores and the drunken troops dragged out everything they could find – barrels of salt meat and fish, wagon-loads of biscuit, clothes, ammunition, medical supplies, the whole equipment of an army – and scattered it all in the streets.

'The kennels were flowing with rum,' a cavalry officer reported, 'a number of puncheons having been staved in the streets, and a promiscuous rabble were drinking and filling bottles and canteens from the stream. Every avenue was crowded with bat-horses, mules and bullock-carts.' 'You could hardly turn round in the place,' another officer said:

> Every corner of it was full of men. And many regiments had to bivouac. Most of the mules and draft-bullocks and pack-horses seemed only to have lasted out up to this point, and now fell down and died. Very soon we

could neither drive nor ride through many of the streets . . . . In the end Villafranca was literally plundered, and the drunkenness that prevailed among the troops led to the most shameful incidents. Down by the river the artillery destroyed all their stores, and lighting big fires burnt all their ammunition wagons, which they broke up for the purpose. They also threw all their ammunition into the river. Several hundred horses which could go no further were led to the same spot and shot. Day and night we could hear the sound of pistol fire. Everything was destroyed. Discipline was at an end.

Moore, who had been with the rearguard, came into the town during the night. The worst excesses were over but the evidence of rioting was plain for him to see. He issued orders that the entire army should parade in the Plaza Major and in the streets leading to it the following morning. By means of threats and promises, curses and appeals, the regiments were brought together at the appointed time in some sort of order. In the middle of the Plaza Major, which was in reality no more than a muddy expanse of waste land bounded by the walls of the town, a stark and crooked tree rose out of the slush-covered earth. Around the tree in long lines the soldiers stood and waited. After a time spent in silence beneath the cold gaze of their General, a detachment of cavalrymen marched on foot through one of the sides of the square of soldiers and took up to the tree a man of their regiment who had plundered a house and struck an officer. The soldier was told to kneel down facing the tree; and the firing squad formed up behind him with their carbines at the ready. In a loud voice the adjutant gave the order to fire and the man fell down at the foot of the tree, shot in the back. The whole army then marched in slow time past his corpse, while Moore himself returned to Cacabelos where the reserve division was becoming almost as unruly as the others. Moore rode up to the men formed up in close columns in a field beside the road and addressed them in what a member of his audience described as a

most formidable and pathetic manner. After dwelling on the outrageous disorder and want of discipline in the army, he concluded by saying: 'And if the enemy are in possession of Bembibre, which I believe, they have got a rare prize. They have taken or cut to pieces many hundred drunken British cowards – for none but unprincipled cowards would get drunk in the presence, nay in the very sight of the enemies of their country: and sooner than survive the disgrace of such infamous conduct, I hope that the first cannon-ball fired by the enemy may take me in the head!' The feeling and pungent address made a deep impression on every individual present, as well officers as men, but the feeling of remorse was but of short duration – future temptations brought on future disorders.

Indeed that very night several houses in Cacabelos were plundered and General Edward Paget decided that the men could not be controlled by a mere appeal to their finer feelings, the existence of which he frequently took leave to doubt.

The Hon. Edward Paget was a remarkable young man. Only a few weeks before he had had his thirty-third birthday, yet he looked as if he had been a general for years. No man had more confidence or a more commanding manner; only Sir David Baird had a more notoriously ill temper. When he gave an order, one of his officers said, 'there was something so peculiar in his glance, so impressive in his tone of voice and so decisive in his manner, that no one held commune, even with himself, as to its propriety or final object'. He had served in Flanders and Holland, in the West Indies, at Gibraltar, in the Egyptian campaign, in Sicily and in Sweden. He had always kept pretty well, he said, 'save and excepting gout, rheumatism, gravel and scurvy'. He could not complain now, he thought, because his eyes were pretty good. And 'in the meantime, to comfort you,' he told his mother, the Countess of Uxbridge, 'my two knees are as big as my head, and I am so rheumatick that I can scarcely move leg or arm, added to which I really and seriously believe I have got gout in my great toe – at least it is very hot, very red, very tender, very painful and very glossy'. He was much addicted to snuff, and believed implicitly in the beneficial effects of flogging.

The morning after General Moore had delivered his 'pungent address' to the men of his division, Paget ordered the regiments to form square beneath the crest of a low hill which would screen them from an advancing enemy. Behind each regiment the criminals were tried by drumhead courts-martial and after being sentenced to the lash were led into the square and tied to triangles formed by sergeants' halberds. As the mournful, hollow-sounding drum-beats tapped out the number of strokes, the soldiers watched the blood pour from the naked, lacerated backs. After each twenty-five strokes the regimental surgeon inspected the wounds to ensure that the victim could survive the next without permanent injury. When the punishment was completed the man was untied, returned to the ranks and another sentenced culprit took his place. For several hours the floggings continued. Frequently vedettes came in to report to General Paget that the enemy was advancing. His only reply was, 'Very well'. The punishments went on.

At last the floggings were all over, and two soldiers convicted of a capital offence were taken to a tree which stood in the square and were lifted up on to the shoulders of men attached to the staff of the provost-marshal. The ends of the ropes, which throughout the morning had been tied round their necks, were thrown over a branch of a tree and fastened there.

The two condemned men watched General Paget, waiting for him to give the signal which would end their lives.

Suddenly, the whole atmosphere of the long drawn-out drama was altered by the abrupt appearance of a *deus ex machina*. General Slade, breathless and red-faced, came galloping into the square to report in a less consequential manner than usual that his picquets were engaged and retiring. General Paget turned on him with that expression of contemptuous anger which he, like Lord Paget, could not conceal in John Slade's presence. 'I am sorry for it, sir,' he said in a voice so loud that his words were distinctly heard all over the field, 'but this information is of a nature which would induce me to expect a report rather by a private dragoon than from you. You had better go back to your fighting picquets, sir, and animate your men to a full discharge of their duty.'

For a few moments after General Slade had galloped off, Paget was silent and appeared to Ensign Blakeney, who was watching the scene with a fearful anxiety, to be 'suffering under great excitement'.

'My God!' shouted Paget at length. 'Is it not lamentable to think that, instead of preparing the troops confided to my command to receive the enemies of their country, I am preparing to hang two robbers? But, though that angle of the square shall be attacked, I shall execute these villains in this angle.'

Again he fell silent, and the waiting soldiers heard the sounds of the picquets retiring up the hill towards them.

'If I spare the lives of these two men,' said Paget, after a pause which had seemed to endure for minutes, 'will you promise to reform?'

Not the slightest sound, not even breathing, was heard within the square. The question was repeated:

'If I spare the lives of these men, will you give me your word of honour as soldiers that you will reform?'

The silence continued, until some officers whispered to their men to say 'Yes'. And so at last the spell was broken and the men shouted out their promise. Hastily the convicted men were untied and lifted down, the triangles were removed, and, as the men gave the cheers they always gave when condemned soldiers were reprieved, the retiring picquets appeared on the summit of the hill and the enemy too were in sight.

The possibility of fighting a delaying action at Cacabelos had been pointed out to Moore by an engineer officer, who on December 26th had sent the General a report in which the difficulties that the French would encounter in trying to turn the position had been emphasised.

The village, he reported, was in a valley through which ran the winding stream of the Cua. The road between Bembibre and Villafranca crossed the Cua by a little stone bridge on either side of which were vineyards enclosed by long hedges and walls running for the most part parallel with the stream. The rising ground on the west side of the stream was ideal for defence.

While the floggings had been carried out below the crest of the hill on the Bembibre side of the stream, a force of about 700 infantry and cavalry provided by the 15th Hussars and the 95th Regiment had acted as a screen along the Bembibre road. It was about one o'clock when these troops fell back over the top of the hill and General Paget allowed the rest of the reserve division to reduce the punishment square and withdraw down the slope towards the bridge. All the regiments crossed the bridge to open out in extended order behind the vineyard walls on the western bank of the river, with the exception of the light company of the 28th Regiment which remained on the enemy side as an escort for a battery of horse artillery. The men were still moving into position when the picquets of the 15th Hussars came galloping down to the bridge, racing past the riflemen of the 95th, many of whom were drunk and were running down the slope with obvious difficulty. Closely behind the hastily retiring picquets came the French 15th Chasseurs and the 3rd Hussars led by General Colbert, a young and dashing officer of astonishing handsomeness.

Within seconds the immediate approaches to the bridge were a confused mass of troops – hussars shouting at the top of their voices; drunken riflemen firing in every direction; French *chasseurs* hacking their way through the *mêlée* and rounding up prisoners. Major Colborne, who had ridden across the bridge with some other officers of the staff to see what was happening at the front, found the enemy suddenly upon him. He was in as great a fright, he confessed, as he had ever been in his life.

> We had to wheel round and ride as hard as we could, and expected them on us every minute. When I saw a Cavalry officer draw his sword, I thought it was high time to draw mine too . . . . We were as nearly as possible taken. We had no idea they were so near . . . . At last we got to the bridge – covered with Rifles, all jammed up on it. We called out 'Go back! Get into the houses! Get into the houses!', and at last we got over. I rode on to the hill, where I was very glad to see the 52nd all drawn up at the foot of the hill. I found Sir John Moore in a great fuss.

And well he might have been. Nearly fifty riflemen were taken prisoner and several hussars had been killed. The light company of the 28th, swamped by the retreating picquets, was unable either to offer any resistance or even to obey the bugle calls to withdraw, for the bridge was completely blocked. To add to Moore's irritation, in the midst of the confusion the energetic General Slade had ridden up to him to make a report which, he said, he had been asked to do by one of his officers, Colonel Grant. Moore looked at Slade with cold disdain and asked him sarcastically how long he had been Colonel Grant's aide-de-camp.

Fortunately the French cavalry had become as disorganised as the reserve division, and General Colbert decided that he would have to pull back and reform his men before making another charge. The few minutes' respite were well spent. The remaining riflemen scrambled across the bridge. The hussars, imperturbably high spirited, bowing low in their saddles like gentlemen at a ball and begging each other ceremoniously to accept the honour of crossing first, trotted after them followed by the light company of the 28th. The 28th quickly took up position beneath the six guns of the horse artillery which opened fire as soon as Colbert charged. Despite the heavy fire, the *chasseurs* and dragoons came on at a fast trot, the round-shot from the horse artillery's guns hurtling down the slope and across the river and bouncing towards them up the hill beyond. Gaps were torn in the head of Colbert's column, which closed up, four abreast, as it approached the bridge and came under the musket fire of the 52nd at the foot of the hill on the opposite side of the river.

The light company of the 28th, waiting below the guns with fixed bayonets, saw the brave French horsemen gallop across the last hundred yards to the bridge and charge furiously across it and up the road towards them. The men of the 52nd and the 95th, kneeling behind the vineyard walls on either side of the road, were able now to deliver a telling cross fire on the flanks of the *chasseurs* as they pounded up towards the guns. Tom Plunkett, an irrepressibly vulgar rifleman of the 95th, took careful aim at General Colbert and brought him crashing to the ground. The men behind him galloped over his corpse and charged into the bayonets of the 28th. But their ranks had been thinned now and their inspiring leader was dead. They fought, sabre to bayonet, for a short time only and then they whirled their horses round and galloped back towards the river. Again they came under that fearful fire from behind the walls and hedges on each side of the road, and many more of them tumbled from their saddles to the ground. One dead *chasseur,* a foot locked in a gilt-spurred stirrup, was dragged through the mud to the river; and his bare, white, wide-eyed head, thumping sickeningly behind a terrified horse, was still remembered forty years later with a horrifying clarity by a young officer who said that nearly all else in that war he had forgotten.

By the time the retreating cavalry reached the river, the road to the bridge, another young officer – Ensign Blakeney of the 28th – reported, 'was absolutely choked with their dead. One alone among the slain was sincerely regretted, their gallant leader, General Colbert; his martial appearance, noble figure, manly gesture, and above all his daring bravery called forth the admiration of all.' His military capacity, however, could be admired by none. His attack, as Robert Blakeney in spite of his regard for Colbert's bravery had to admit, 'was most ill-advised, ill-judged, and seemingly without any final object in view'. It was true that his men's

> bravery was too obvious to be doubted; but they rushed on reckless of all opposition, whether apparent or probable, and had they succeeded in cutting through the light company, which they would have found some difficulty in doing, and although they would then have escaped the cross-fire of the 95th, yet they would have been in a worse position than before. When they had passed beyond the light company a hundred yards they would have encountered the left wing of the 28th Regiment, supported, if necessary, by the right wing directly on their flank, although a little in their rear, and had their number, which was but from four to five hundred men, been quadrupled, every man must have been shot, bayoneted, or taken prisoner.

Of more consequence to the enemy, however, than the loss of 200 horsemen was the galvanic effect that shooting them had upon the men of the reserve division. Thoughts of drink and plunder were put aside now. They had fought the enemy and they had won and they wanted only to live to fight him again. It had been an exhilarating experience. They did not have long to wait before they were given another opportunity of proving their worth. Soon after Colbert's charge had been repulsed, the French cavalry made another attempt to cut through the British position. This time, having found a ford well downstream from the bridge, they splashed through the Cua and supported by a battalion of *tirailleurs* advanced against the right of the position. The 95th ran back from the walls and hedges which lined the road and were soon heavily engaged. As more French troops crossed the stream and began to push the riflemen back, the 52nd Regiment, which had been previously withdrawn by Moore from the left of the position to the centre, came down in support of the British right.

General Merle, who was directing the French attack from the hill where the British punishment squares had stood that morning, had seen the movements of the 52nd and understood that Moore was concerned lest the flanks of that regiment should be turned. Taking advantage of the now undefended ground on the British left, Merle launched an attack on that side also. As the heads of his columns approached the river, the guns of the horse artillery were pulled round and laid in their direction. The gunners held their fire until they could not miss and then all six guns opened up together with devastating effect. The massed columns halted immediately, then broke, then fled. And the cavalry and *voltigeurs* on the right soon afterwards fell back too. They galloped and ran back through the stream with the 95th and 52nd cheering wildly as they chased after them, their muskets and rifles flashing and their bayonets dripping blood. The men, in fact, were so excited now that their officers could not hold them back. They were 'so wild and hot for the fray', one of their officers reported with pride, 'that it was hard to drag them from the field. Indeed, it was more difficult to withdraw our men from the fight than to loose the hold of a highbred mastiff.'

It was not until darkness fell that the sounds of firing died away. By then rather more than 200 men on each side had been killed; but the men of the reserve division did not doubt that they had won a great victory. They continued their retreat to Villafranca in a spirit almost of gaiety. It was snowing again and the cold was intense, but one of them felt more braced than benumbed by it. 'We pressed forward,' he said, 'like soldiers upon whom the light of conviction had flashed and to whom physical powers were not wanting, and so marched that night to Herrerias, a distance of eighteen miles, and if I mistake not, without leaving a single straggler of our division behind.'

On the way they passed through Villafranca where fires sent showers of sparks and billows of dense smoke into the dark, snow-clouded sky. The army had left and only the commissaries remained to ensure that no supplies remained undestroyed to fall into the hands of the enemy. So anxious, indeed, were the commissaries to carry out their orders to the letter, that they refused to let the hungry men of the reserve help themselves from the piles of unburned salt meat and biscuit as they marched past. Everything must be destroyed, they said, and they asked the officers to ensure that their men took nothing. But the men paid no attention to so curious a restriction and, as the barrels of salt pork were pushed into the flames, they jabbed their bayonets through the broken sides and brought out great hunks of meat which they carried on their shoulders to Herrerias.

8

Villafranca to Lugo

'A comparison drawn at this period between the British army and Romana's mob would not have been much in favour of the former.
Captain Alexander Gordon, 15th Hussars

IN FRONT OF the reserve division, the 'clodhoppers', as the light infantry disdainfully called them, were continuing their retreat in agony and despair. Beyond Villafranca the road wound its desolate way across the Cantabrian mountains, through the defile of Piedrafita, and up the spurs of Monte Cebrero to the barren upland plain of Lugo. These sixty miles were the worst of the whole retreat. 'All the straggling and irregularities that had occurred on any former occasion', Captain Gordon thought,

> might be considered as perfection of discipline if compared with the retreat from Villafranca which resembled the flight of an indisciplined rabble rather than the march of regular troops; and a comparison drawn at this period between the British army and Romana's mob would not have been much in favour of the former.

It was not only drunkards and sick men who fell out now and wandered off to give themselves up to the French or to lie down and die in the snow. Many of the best and most conscientious soldiers could not keep up with the others and stumbled and slumped to the ground, to be found later by the rearguard frozen hard to the snow. A soldier of the 71st, barefoot and limping, afterwards confessed he was obsessed by the temptation to give in and find relief from his agony in death. 'The road was one line of bloody foot-marks, from the sore feet of the men; and on its sides were the dead and dying. Human nature could do no more.' He had only been prevented from abandoning himself to the snow by the encouragement of the rough Highlander who was his friend. But now the Highlander too was failing.

> He as well as myself had long been bare-footed and lame; he that encouraged me to proceed, now himself lay down to die. For two days he

had been almost blind and unable from a severe cold to hold up his head. We sat down together; not a word escaped our lips. We looked round – then at each other, and closed our eyes. I attempted to pray, and recommend myself to God; but my mind was so confused I could not arrange my ideas. I almost think I was deranged.

When he felt himself sinking into either sleep or death, however, he heard shouts and firing. It was an advance party of the French who had caught up with the stragglers. Scarcely conscious of what he was doing, he got to his feet, fired his musket and watched the French dragoons wheel about and trot away. He turned about himself and limped on again, his footprints marking the snow with fresh blood. The blood on the beaten track, which seemed to stretch without end in front of him, came not only from the bare feet of the men but from the horses too. For the roughness of the road, hardened by frost, had caused most of the horses to cast their shoes, and the supplies of nails and shoes in the forge carts had long since given out. 'It was no uncommon sight', one old cavalry soldier noted with pity, 'to witness the poor animals ridden with the blood gushing from their hoofs.'

But for most pity was an emotion which they could no longer feel. They had gone beyond compassion to the deadness of despair. They marched on, unthinking and unfeeling. They watched friends fall to the ground and they left them there; they ate secret stores of food alone and in concealment; they looked at men who still had shoes and their eyes seemed to say, 'If you were dead those shoes would be mine'; they looked at women dragging their half-dead children after them through the snow and had neither strength nor will to help them. Once Commissary Schaumann saw a woman fall up to her waist in a bog and as she was sucked down by the slimy, ice-cold water, the men behind her walked over her head.

There were not many women left now. Most of them, too ill or weak or drunk to carry on, had been left behind and had died by the roadside or had dragged themselves off to a mountain hut. And one night in a hut near Nogales a patrol of enemy dragoons had found three women and taken it in turns to rape them, and then left them there to die. But some women survived the cold and hunger, pain and exhaustion to struggle on beside their men, looking 'like a tribe of travelling beggars', Rifleman Harris thought, with enormous greatcoats buttoned up over their heads and the rest of their scanty, ragged clothing not reaching low enough to conceal their naked legs. A few of them were pregnant. One of them, a sturdy and hard Irishwoman, fell to the back of her husband's column when the contractions warned her that the child was coming. Not long afterwards she caught up with the regiment again and took it in turns with her husband to carry the baby to the coast and put him aboard a ship for England where he grew up strong and healthy. Other mothers, however, could not survive the shock of so comfortless a labour. Surgeon Griffith passed one lying dead in the snow with her baby sucking frantically at her frozen breast; and he stopped to pick up the baby and wrapping it up he strapped it to his saddle. One of Moore's staff officers found another baby in an overturned bullock cart and rolled it in his cloak and rode away with it. The mother was frozen to death and the bullocks, still yoked to the wagon in which she had been carried, lay under the shafts too exhausted to rise.

Dead and dying mules and bullocks lay everywhere. One officer calculated that, on every ten miles of road, 100 animals lay dead. Only the guns were saved. Even the Paymaster-General's carts had to be abandoned when the bullocks collapsed beneath the weight of the coin. A soldier was left guarding barrels full of silver dollars to the value of £25,000 'and with a desperate air implored every officer that passed', so one of them said, 'to relieve him of his duty'. The Assistant Paymaster-General himself rode back to the reserve to beg help of General Paget. He could not have found a less sympathetic audience.

'Pray, sir,' asked the nervous paymaster of an officer of the division, 'where is General Paget?'

As Paget was less than five yards away from him, the officer thought 'it would be indecorous' to make a reply. The paymaster repeated the question. The officer remained silent. General Paget pushed himself away from the wall against which he had been leaning, and putting on his hat, said in a loud and menacing voice, 'I am General Paget, sir. Pray what are your demands?'

'Oh, beg pardon, sir. I am Paymaster-General, and . . .'

'Alight, sir!'

The paymaster nervously did so, and continued: 'The treasure of the army, sir, is close in the rear, and the bullocks being jaded are unable to proceed; I therefore want fresh animals to draw it forward.'

'Pray, sir, do you take me for a bullock driver or a muleteer, or knowing who I am have you the presence of mind coolly to tell me that through a total neglect or ignorance of your duty you are about to lose the treasure of the army committed to your charge? . . . Had you the slightest conception of your duty,' General Paget went on, working himself into a fury of rage and ignoring the French advance guard who were in full view in the valley below, as he delivered himself of his violent and vociferous reprimand, 'you would have known that you ought to be a day's march ahead of the whole army, instead of hanging back with your confounded bullocks and carts upon the rearmost company of the rearguard . . . . What, sir! To come to me and impede my march with your carts, and ask me to look for bullocks when I should be free from all encumbrances and my mind occupied by no other care than that of disposing my troops to the best advantage in resisting the approaching enemy! It is doubtful, sir, whether your conduct can be attributed to ignorance and neglect alone.'

By this time the enemy had begun to engage the rearguard and musket balls were flying through the air, but the General had not finished yet. The officer who had overheard the speech, however, was now too distracted to concentrate on it any further, and the only other words he remembered from its closing passages were 'ought to be hanged!' Having given this final verdict on the unfortunate paymaster, General Paget turned his attention to the French who had managed to creep round his right flank. He extricated his men with his usual dexterity and came again upon the paymaster who had managed at last to get his carts into painfully slow and creaking motion.

General Paget did not for a moment suppose that the paymaster could succeed in getting them away from the enemy. He ordered Lieutenant Bennet of the 28th Regiment to have the casks thrown over the side of the road into the abyss below and to shoot the first man who attempted to touch the dollars inside them. Not a man moved forward as the casks were pushed over the precipice and went hurtling down on to the rocks to be shattered there instantly. The silver coins flew from the broken wood and cascaded over the snow at the bottom of the valley in a glittering shower.

Several dollars had spilt from the casks as they had been lifted from the wagons, but the men did not dare to stoop to pick them up; and the French dragoons who came trotting down the road a few minutes later stopped and filled their pockets before continuing their advance. But when the General's back was turned several men lagged behind and clambered down into the valley to search for the treasure so unfeelingly thrown away. Mrs. Maloney, wife of the 52nd Regiment's master-tailor, was one of those who succeeded in reaching the treasure and concealing about her voluminous clothing a fortune in silver dollars which she struggled to carry away with her. Later on, however, some squadrons of the 15th Hussars took a more reasonable view of the value of money to men who were living on the verge of death. They had been supplied with sealed bags, containing 500 dollars each, which the Commissariat had been unable to move from Lugo; but the bags were heavy and their horses weak and so they untied the bags from their saddles and hurled them into the night. To throw away more money than they had ever seen before would, one of them supposed, have seemed an impossible action a few weeks ago. But nothing was quite real any more. They trotted on through the interminable wastes of snow in unaccustomed silence, hearing only the muffled chink of scabbard and spurs beneath their long cloaks.

And they were the lucky ones. Trailing behind them were the men on foot, staggering forward 'amid a deep silence which was broken only by the howling of the storm and the groans of those who flung themselves left and right on to the ground, never to rise again'. Money counted for nothing here. Rich officers limped at the heads of their companies, destitute of shoes and stockings, with their clothes in rags. 'I have seen officers of the guards', said a private in the 71st, 'and others, worth thousands, with pieces of old blanket wrapt round their feet; the men pointing at them, with a malicious satisfaction, saying, "There goes three thousand a year!" '

The men would not have been so bitter, another soldier thought, if the officers had let them stand and fight. They could not understand the retreat. They had not lost a battle. They had not even fought one. Every time a group of stragglers made a stand, the enemy fell back. They would rather 'face a hundred fresh Germans than ten dying Englishmen', one of them had heard a Frenchman say, so why not turn and give them a thrashing? Sometimes there were rumours that Sir John would take the next opportunity to make a stand. But as each time the men 'saw the most favourable ground for defensive operations abandoned without even a show of resistance', Captain Gordon said that they 'lost all confidence in a General who neglected to seize and improve opportunities which every private soldier was capable of appreciating'.

There was, for a moment, a brief hope in the reserve division that a stand would be made at the village of Constantino where high ground commanded the approaches to a bridge across a narrow, but fast-flowing stream. The infantry and artillery had been well placed here by Moore himself and they waited in confidence for the expected attack. They were well, if outlandishly, clothed; for during the previous night they had plundered a caravan of carts containing uniforms and shoes for Romana's army. Some men wore grey trousers, some wore blue. Others wore white breeches and white shoes, or one black shoe and one white. Lieutenant Cadell, a very tall officer of the 28th, cut a hole for his head in a blanket and wore that, looking like the shepherds his men were later to see striding across the mountains on stilts. The enemy may have been led to imagine, a fellow officer thought, that they were facing Spanish troops. But after three successive rushes which they vainly made, cavalry and infantry uniting to force their way over the bridge, they returned each time under a thorough conviction that they had been received by British troops alone'. But, despite the ease with which the tentative French attacks were repulsed, at nightfall the position was abandoned; and the reserve was ordered back again.

It was becoming 'more like a shameful flight' than a planned retreat, a soldier afterwards wrote in exasperation. The army had begun to believe that 'Moore would never fight . . . . We all wished it but none believed it'. Many officers agreed with their men. Mr. Crabb Robinson, preparing material for his last despatches in Corunna, was soon to be given evidence of their bitterness. 'The retreat was more properly a flight', they told him. 'It was conducted very blunderingly and with precipitation.'

There were blunders, it was true. In his single criticism of the whole campaign Wellington afterwards said that Moore ought, in anticipation of his retreat, 'to have sent officers to the rear to mark and prepare the halting-places for every brigade'. It was a justified comment. Wellington, however, might also have said that the officers sent to perform these duties during the early part of the retreat had proved utterly incapable of them and Moore had decided that it would be no use sending others. The general incompetence of staff officers, in fact, was in the words of an intelligent young cavalry captain 'one of the chief causes of the miseries suffered by the army during the retreat'. The ignorance displayed by the staff and Commissariat was 'quite inexcusable', and 'appeared more manifestly from the different manner in which the duties of these departments are conducted in the French army'.

It was not only staff officers who were culpable. Many regimental officers, too, displayed an incompetence equally disastrous and made mistakes no less damaging. Some of these mistakes were inevitable. One blunder, however, committed by Sir David Baird on January 6th was not.

On that day Moore was handed a report from his chief engineer, Colonel Fletcher. For several days the General had been trying to decide upon a port for the embarkation of his army. He had considered following the light brigades to Vigo; he had considered also the possibility of Ferrol as an alternative to Corunna. The navy did not like the idea of Corunna; he himself did not favour Vigo, as there was no position in front of it from which he could cover the embarkation. But he deferred his decision until he received the report of his engineer. Fletcher had been to Vigo, Betanzos, Corunna and Ferrol, and on the night of January 5th read his report to Major Colborne who listened 'half asleep with fatigue'. Early next morning the report was given to Moore who accepted the advice it contained and gave orders for the army to make for Corunna.

George Napier galloped off to the leading divisions, whose existing orders were to take the Vigo road on reaching Lugo. The first division Napier met was Baird's at Nogales. Sir David was in bed and greeted

Napier with an ill-temper which had now become habitual. He read the despatch with growing irritation, for he had always strongly advocated the choice of Vigo as a place to re-embark. When he had finished, he asked Napier if he was going to take it on to General Fraser and to John Hope. Napier replied that he had no instructions to do so but that, if Sir David had no officer of his own he could send, he would willingly go on himself. All he needed was a horse. The suggestion seemed to make the General crosser than ever. If those were Napier's orders well and good, he could return to Headquarters. A dragoon orderly would be sent on with Sir John Moore's letter. Nervously George Napier ventured to suggest that the instructions contained in the letter were extremely important and he was very willing to ride on himself, rather than let an orderly go.

'Sir!' said Baird, in a voice which brooked no denial. 'Sir! That is my business. I shall send it by a dragoon.'

And so he did. But the letter never arrived. The dragoon got drunk and lost it. The leading regiments of Fraser's division had gone nearly ten miles down the difficult road to Vigo before they were recalled; and on the march back to Lugo 400 stragglers were left behind.

When the rest reached Lugo, however, they were given news which eased their savage temper.

9

Lugo to Betanzos

'I must confess that some even of the reserve, absolutely exhausted from the exertions they used in arousing the slothful of other divisions to a sense of their duty, could not resist the temptation . . . . and they too remained behind.'

Ensign Robert Blakeney, 28th Regiment

THE GENERAL had decided to make a stand at Lugo. The prospect of a battle, however, pleased his men and his staff more than it pleased himself.

'Well, Sir John,' Colonel Graham had said when he heard the satisfactory news, 'after we have beaten them you will take us on in pursuit of them a few days, won't you?'

'No,' Moore said decisively, 'I have had enough of Galicia.'

'Oh!' Graham persisted. 'But just a few days after them you must take us.'

Moore did not reply.

His face these last few days, Graham had noticed, was that of a man worn down by disappointment and despair. He had lost faith in his army. He would not have believed, he confessed, that British troops could behave so badly. The reserve division was fighting well now; but the rest of the infantry were a disgrace. He knew what many officers were saying of him. He knew that at Astorga, at Villafranca, at Constantino, there had been complaints and grumbles, criticism and abuse. He realised that at each of these places a theoretical case might be put for making a stand. But as soon as he halted he ran the risk of being outflanked on the north by a force advancing through the Asturias from Oviedo, or on the south by an advance up the Minho valley from Orense. The best information he could get was that an enemy army moving in either direction would have to pass through mountains scarcely accessible even in summer; but he had grown used to distrusting the advice of Spanish officers. In any event, even if the dangers of being outflanked were discounted, he refused to agree that any benefit would come of placing 20,000 troops in however strong a position and offering battle to an enemy with 300,000 men in Spain. It might look well in the eyes of the world; but he could be of more use to the Spaniards if he saved the only force they had left for their protection, by getting it safely to the sea and fighting another day when the odds were not so heavily against him. Above all, he doubted the wisdom of fighting the French with an army which, as he despairingly told Lord Castlereagh, had 'totally changed its character since it began to retreat . . . . I can', Moore added, 'say nothing in its favour, but that, when there was a prospect of fighting the Enemy, the men were then orderly, and seemed pleased and determined to do their duty.'

It was then, more with the hope that the men would pull themselves together if a fight were in view than that the French would oblige him by an attack, that Moore decided to defend the hills at Lugo. He did not want to be unduly provocative, nor did he intend to wait for an attack too long; but the ground was strong and the stores at Lugo contained both food and ammunition. He arrived in the little town on January 6th and at once issued a General Order which increased the mutterings of those regimental officers who had already decided that his censure of them was as unjust as his conduct of the campaign was ill-judged:

> Generals and commanding officers of Corps must be as sensible as the Commander of the Forces, of the complete disorganisation of the army, . . . The Commander of the Forces is tired of giving orders which are never attended to: he therefore appeals to the honour and feelings of the army he commands; and if those are not sufficient to induce them to do their duty, he must despair of succeeding by any other means. He was forced to order one soldier to be shot at Villa Franca, and he will order all others to be executed who are guilty of similar enormities; but he considers that there would be no occasion to proceed to such extremities if the officers did their duty; as it is chiefly from their negligence, and from want of proper regulations in the regiments, that crimes and irregularities are committed, in quarters and upon the march.

But if some officers had given up trying to check the abuses of the men on the march, they had, now that a battle was offered, no cause for resignation or despair. 'Every order was obeyed with alacrity', one officer wrote. 'And not a trace remained of the discontent and insubordination which had been so general for the past few days.'

The recent blinding, soaking rain had given way to a cold more intense even than before; and the stocks of food at Lugo were not as plentifully distributed as the men had been led to hope they would be. But a mood almost of cheerfulness came over the troops as they looked down from the hills to the valley below, across which the French would have to move to the attack. They were provided with pipe clay from the Lugo stores and ordered to whiten their belts and polish their buttons, and even this order was obeyed with little more than the usual grumbling which, on active service, it habitually evoked.

The most unobservant and unintelligent soldier could not but admire the strength of the British position. The gently sloping valley below them was broken up by dry stone walls and the hedges of winding lanes; and the opposing heights where the French were gathering were more than a mile away. On the right the position was bounded by the unfordable Minho river and on the left by inaccessible hills.

Major-General Leith's brigade, from Baird's division, had retreated too far in December to be recalled to take part in the advance to Sahagun and had been retreating at a leisurely pace on Lugo where it was able to increase Moore's force by 1,800 fresh men. Sending the light brigades to Lugo, however, had reduced his army by nearly twice that number; and 2,000 more men had been lost during the last ten days of retreat. Between 500 and 600 sick, too ill to move, had been left behind in the buildings used as hospitals at Astorga and Villafranca. A thousand cavalrymen whose horses had died had been sent back to Corunna on foot. The total number of combatants available at Lugo were thus no more than 18,000. But although so few they were confident that when the French attacked they would defeat them.

The confidence did not seem misplaced. On the day after his arrival at Lugo, Soult was given an unexpected jolt. During the morning of January 7th, he began to prod the British position, believing that his leading regiments had probably once more come up against General Paget's rearguard which they would soon be able to push back. He brought up a battery to open fire on the apparent centre of the position, intending to send four squadrons of cavalry through the gap which the guns would open up for him. But the reply to his battery's first few shots was shattering. Fifteen guns blazed out from the mountains, and the French battery was immediately silenced. An hour later, he felt for the left and right of the position by making a feint opposite the Guards on the right and sending a column of infantry supported by five guns against the left. The tentative attack on the left was at first successful. The outposts of Leith's brigade, against which it was directed, fell back up the lower slopes in disorder; and for a time it seemed that the French infantry might break through. Moore himself rode up, accompanied by some officers of his staff and the wife of Colonel M'kenzie of the 5th, who seemed not at all put out to find herself under fire. The General, shouting encouragement to the men and riding up and down amongst them, soon rallied them and sent them hurtling down with bayonets fixed against the advancing infantry. The charge led by General Leith himself at the head of the 59th

was so well done and the pursuit so energetically led that between three
and four hundred enemy infantrymen did not succeed in regaining their
lines.

By the early evening all French troops had been withdrawn and Soult
had decided to wait until his numbers were reinforced by the regiments
still on the march from Constantino. Here British engineers had failed in
their attempts to destroy the bridge and every hour more of his troops
were crossing the river. On the morning of January 8th over 20,000 men
had joined him and fifty guns were in battery to support their attack.
Acting as Moore constantly feared he would do, he sent an order back
to Ney to detach a division of the 6th Corps by the Val des Orres to
Orense and so outrank the English on their right.

For the whole of that day, Moore anxiously waited for the French to
attack. Under a sky the colour of wet slate his men looked across to the
French lines, searching eagerly for a sign of activity. There was none.
When night fell the whole dark day had been spent in silence.

At nine o'clock the order to retire was given. There was not enough
food left for Moore to wait another day. To take the initiative himself
would be absurd; for he was outnumbered now and the French position
although not as strong as his own was strong enough. A defeat would be
disastrous, a victory impossible to exploit. The best that he could hope
for was to creep away unobserved and to gain a few hours' start on his
pursuers.

The men knew nothing of this and they were not told. Between
half-past nine and ten o'clock they withdrew, grumbling and cursing,
from their positions. It was a fearful night, black and tempestuous. The
storm clouds had burst and a howling wind blew the sleet and rain into
their faces and through their clothes, and lifted and scattered the piles of
straw which had been placed to mark the withdrawal routes. Amidst the
winding lanes and the criss-cross of stone walls on the westerly slopes of
the mountain, officers got lost and took their almost mutinous men for
miles in the wrong direction. For the rest of that night separated
companies, straggling battalions and whole brigades wandered about
helplessly on the mountain-side until, when daylight came and the
commanders found their bearings at last, the exhausted troops tumbled
into the village of Valmeida and sank down disconsolately in the mud to
eat what bits of sodden biscuit they could scrape from the inside of their
haversacks. The rain still poured down and some compassionate officers
allowed their men to break their ranks and seek the protection of nearby
barns, where they fell on to the dry straw and were immediately so fast
asleep that even the kicks of their sergeants could not rouse them.

After less than an hour's rest the army moved on again and at one o'clock the leading regiment entered 'a dirty miserable-looking village called Guitoriez' in the midst of the most violent storm of hail and rain that at least one of its officers had ever witnessed. About 200 cavalry horses found shelter in a large stable at the *posada,* but the riders were obliged to crowd into the kitchen and passages as all the other rooms were occupied by Sir David Baird, his staff and officers. Captain Gordon of the 15th Hussars found a place near the fire 'round which a number of officers and men of different corps were assembled to dry their clothes and thaw their half-frozen limbs'. But they were 'soon disturbed by Sir David Baird's cook, who insisted upon having the fire entirely to herself that she might boil his tea-kettle. She was so violently enraged' when the men refused to get out of her way, that she did not stop cursing them until she was 'quite out of breath'.

While the leading divisions waited in the teeming rain at Guitiriz for the stragglers and reserve division to close up with them, all the houses in the village, and all the few remaining commissariat wagons, were plundered by the ravenous troops. Some casks of wine were found and a cart load of salt fish and rum, and the men fell upon them like wolves. The combination of raw salt fish and rum 'in empty stomachs', said Commissary Schaumann,

> resulted in the death of many of the men on the spot, while several others went mad. One of them took up a defiant attitude, *à la* Fabius, in the middle of the road, and with fixed bayonet shouted that he was General Moore; that the army was to halt, turn round and give battle. And by standing there with legs wide apart, in the middle of the road, brandishing his bayonet, he barred the way to me, a colonel, and several other officers. When at last coaxing words proved of no avail, the whole lot of us crashed forward and rode over him.

Such drastic remedies were found to be necessary too by the reserve division which had been left behind once again to form the rearguard and to bring up the stragglers, hundreds of whom had wandered out of the ranks almost delirious with exhaustion. Many fell down by the roadside where, unable to keep awake any longer, they closed their eyes never again to open them; others stumbled into barns and roadside cottages and hid there until the men of the rearguard came beating on the doors and tumbled them out at the point of the bayonet. But as often as not, Robert Blakeney of the 28th reported, the men could not be moved:

> We kicked, thumped, struck with the butt ends of our firelocks, pricked with swords and bayonets, but to little purpose. And here I must confess

that some even of the reserve, absolutely exhausted from the exertions they used in arousing the slothful of other divisions to a sense of their duty . . . could not resist the temptation; and in the partial absence of the officers, who were rousing up other stragglers, sat and from that sunk down probably with the intention of taking only a few minutes repose; yet they too remained behind.

Those stragglers, however, who could be got out again on to the road, turned round when their pursuers got too close and fought them back with that reckless, desperate bravery that had by now earned them the reputation of '*les squellettes féroces*'. On one occasion a sergeant of the 5th, so weak from diarrhoea that he had felt obliged to join some other men for a few hours' rest in a barn, was woken up by the sound of carbine fire. 'Some of the men jumped up,' he wrote,

> ran out, discharged their pieces and were shot dead on the spot. To surrender was the prevailing opinion. 'Let us just see them first', said I. 'They may be but a few, and we are too many to be frightened.' On looking through an aperture in the wall, I saw at about a hundred yards from the building eight or ten dragoons drawn up. We were seven men, and a drummer who was unable to move, and we agreed to defend ourselves.

They rushed out into the road and opened fire as the dragoons charged at them and ran them down. Two of them were killed; but when the rest were taken prisoner and marched roughly away, two dragoons also lay dead behind them.

Later on that day four or five hundred stragglers were trailing along wearily behind the reserve when they were overtaken by a private of the 28th Regiment leading an exhausted mule. The soldier – batman to Surgeon Dacres, whose heavy medical panniers strapped to the sides of the mule had slowed the animal down to a laboriously ambling pace – heard the sound of trotting hooves behind him and looked over his shoulder to see several squadrons of Polish lancers moving down the road. He shouted a warning to the stragglers and with wonderful spirit and energy succeeded in getting them to form up into some sort of square. Several of them were cut down by the lancers before they could join the square but the rest formed up and opened fire on the cavalry and kept them at bay. Handing over his command to a sergeant the batman calmly continued his journey up the road with Surgeon Dacres's mule, occasionally turning round to watch the stragglers holding their ground as more and more French troops came up to oppose them. With extraordinary skill the British soldiers withdrew in detachments up the road while others gave them covering fire, until all of them had reached the rearguard.

General Paget was not, however, disposed to pardon them. He had watched the engagement from the top of the hill and when his men showed that they wanted to advance against the cavalry below he said that he would not risk the life of even one good soldier to save a 'whole horde of those drunken marauders'.

He had a guard put across the road and as each straggler came up his pack was taken off and he was closely searched. All the money taken from the pockets of these men was put in a pile and distributed to the soldiers of the reserve who had not lagged behind their colours. The rest of the loot was put in another pile and young Ensign Blakeney, as yet unfamiliar with the British soldiers' peculiar passion for useless plunder, was amazed at the sight of it. 'It is impossible to enumerate the different articles', he wrote. 'Brass candlesticks bent double, bundles of common knives, copper saucepans hammered into masses, every sort of domestic utensil which could be forced into their packs, were found upon them without any regard as to value or weight.'

Blakeney said that no less than 1,500 stragglers ambled sullenly through the rearguard that day to join their respective regiments on the road to Betanzos. A fellow officer thought that 'straggling had increased to such a degree, that if the retreat had continued three days longer the army must have been totally annihilated'. Certainly it seems that William Napier was right when he suggested that the march from Lugo to Betanzos cost the army in stragglers more than double the number of men lost in all the preceding operations. For, although growing weaker and more hungry with every mile, the soldiers were required to march at a pace which would have exhausted fit men straight from England. 'We came down from the hills more dead than alive', a soldier remembered. 'If it had not been for the promise of food when we got down to the sea, we would never have done it.'

But on January 10th he reached Betanzos and over the hill was the sea and the winding road to Corunna.

10

Astorga to Vigo

'No man but one formed of stuff like General Craufurd could have saved the brigade from perishing altogether. I detest the sight of the lash; but I am convinced the British army can never go on without it.'

Rifleman Harris, 95th Regiment

THE 3,500 MEN of the light brigades were still on march to Vigo. Detached from the main army at Astorga to keep it safe from attack on its southern flank, as well as to lessen the strain on the resources of the Commissariat, they had marched in conditions of even severer hardship. The regiments that composed these two brigades were good ones and had a lower proportion of criminals and loafers than many others in which one in every seven or eight men was a drunkard, a malingerer, or a thief. But the route across the mountains and through the bleak Minho valley was a terrible one; the weather was appalling and food scarce. Many soldiers afterwards admitted that they only survived through the iron determination of their brigadiers that they should do so.

Karl Alten, who commanded the brigade formed by the regiments of the King's German Legion, had been commissioned in the Hanoverian Guards at the age of seventeen and had made a name for himself before he was thirty as a brilliant commander of light infantry. When the Hanoverian Army was disbanded in 1803, he had gone to England where both the Duke of York and Moore had soon recognised his talents. He was brave and energetic; and, more unusual in a German, capable both of enforcing strict discipline amongst his troops and of winning their affection. This capacity to command obedience through both fear and sympathy, rare indeed among generals of any race, was also a notable characteristic of Robert Craufurd, his fellow brigade commander whose regiments were the 1st Battalion of the 43rd Regiment, the 2nd/52nd and the 2nd/95th.

Colonel Craufurd was, perhaps, the most remarkable of all the Peninsular generals. A forty-four-year-old Scotsman, short and thick with dark, restless eyes and nervously agitated movements, he had a temper as fierce as Sir David Baird's and a tongue even more caustically fluent than

Edward Paget's. He had made many enemies. But even they – although the days of his greatest achievements were still ahead of him – had to agree that '"Black Bob" knew what he was talking about'. Before he was twenty he had completed a thorough study of the tactics of Frederick the Great; before he was thirty he had been appointed military attaché to the Austrian army in the Netherlands; and before he was forty he had earned the reputation of being one of the best informed speakers on military topics in Parliament where he sat as a member for East Retford, a pocket borough in the gift of the Dowager Duchess of Newcastle who had married his brother. He was as skilful in the practice of war, as he was learned in its theory; and although he frequently treated his officers like stupid children and his men like animals, the behaviour of both after his funeral gave eloquent testimony to the admiration they had had for him. He died in 1812, four days after he had been wounded directing the stormers of the Light Division on the glacis of Ciudad Rodrigo. His men marched back to their lines, having buried him in the breach of the fortress, and on the way they came up against one of the siege works which had flooded with water. It had been one of the General's most fervently held opinions that his troops should never make a detour to avoid walking through a fordable stream. There was scarcely a moment's hesitation before the leading files marched into the deep water and the men behind followed them without question.

On the retreat to Vigo he had made it immediately plain that he would tolerate no diversions and no evasions. On one occasion, as his brigade led the way into Ponferrada, he noticed some men running down a river bank to find a bridge so as to avoid walking through water which would have reached their waists. He ordered them back, had all of them flogged and sent them through the river at the deepest place he could find. On another occasion he saw an officer being carried through a river on the back of one of his men. He splashed through the river after him, radiating fury. 'Put him down, sir! Put him down!' he shouted. 'I desire you to put that officer down instantly.' And when the man had 'dropped his burden like a hot potato into the stream' Craufurd in his loud and ferocious voice ordered the officer to go back to the bank and start all over again. Another officer, who as Sergeant Surtees said 'was not very well', tried to avoid walking through the river and by way of punishment was made to walk backwards and forwards from bank to bank repeatedly.

'No man but one formed of stuff like General Craufurd could have saved the brigade from perishing altogether', Rifleman Harris said. 'I detest the sight of the lash; but I am convinced the British army can never go on without it.' By using the lash without compunction on any man guilty of the least sign of insubordination, Harris thought, Craufurd saved the lives of hundreds. The young rifleman gave an example of the brigadier's severity which throws a vivid light both on Craufurd's character and that of the men whose discipline he was so determined to preserve:

> I remember one evening he detected two men straying away from the main body; it was in the early stages of that disastrous flight, and Craufurd knew well that he must keep his division together. He halted the brigade with a voice of thunder, ordered a drum-head court martial on the instant, and they were sentenced to a hundred apiece. While this hasty trial was taking place Craufurd, dismounting from his horse, stood in the midst, looking stern and angry as a worried bulldog. He did not like retreating at all, that man.
>
> The three men nearest him, as he stood, were Jagger, Dan Howans and myself. All were worn, dejected and savage, though nothing to what we were after a few days more of the retreat. The whole brigade was in a grumbling and discontented mood; and Craufurd, doubtless, felt ill-pleased with the aspect of affairs altogether.
>
> 'Damn his eyes!' muttered Howans. 'He had much better try to get us something to eat and drink than harass us in this way.'

Craufurd overheard Howan's whispered words and, beside himself with rage, turned round on the three men and snatching one of their rifles brought the butt-end crashing down on Jagger's head.

'I heard you, sir,' said Craufurd, 'and I will bring you also to a court-martial.'

'It wasn't I who spoke', Jagger said, getting up and shaking his head, as he added with an injured sulkiness, 'You shouldn't knock me about.'

Rifleman Howans then admitted that it was he who had spoken.

'Very well', replied Craufurd, without looking again at Jagger. 'Then I will try you, sir.'

Howans was tried and sentenced to three hundred lashes. But it was dark now and the punishment could not be inflicted. So Craufurd gave the order to the brigade to move on, and all that night he marched in the ranks on foot. In the morning his hair, beard and eyebrows were covered with frost so that he looked as if he had grown white with age. At dawn he brought the brigade to a halt and, ordering it to form a square, he had Howans and the two other men who had been sentenced the night before brought into the middle of it to face him.

'Although I should obtain the ill-will of the men of the brigade by so doing,' he announced, 'I am resolved to punish these three men according to the sentence awarded even though the French are at our heels. Begin with Daniel Howans.'

As the regiments of the light brigade carried no halberds there was some difficulty in finding a place for the drummers to tie Howans up, but eventually they found a lone ash tree and led him to that.

'Don't trouble yourselves about tying me up', said Howans, folding his arms. 'I'll take my punishment like a man.'

'He did so without a murmur,' Harris remembered,

> receiving the whole three hundred. His wife, who was present with us, was a strong, hardy Irishwoman. When it was over, she stepped up and covered Howans with his grey great-coat. The general then gave the word to move on. I rather think he knew the enemy was too near to punish the two other delinquents just then; so we proceeded out of the cornfield in which we had been halted, and toiled away upon the hills once more. Howan's wife carrying the jacket, knapsack and pouch, which the lacerated state of the man's back would not permit him to bear.

The brigade, however, had only been marching for another hour when again it was halted, and Craufurd said, 'Bring out the two men of the 95th who were tried last night'.

The men were brought up to him, and their commanding officer, Lieutenant-Colonel Hamilton Wade, came up with them. The Colonel lowered his sword and requested that Craufurd would forgive his two men as they were good soldiers at heart and had fought well in all the battles of Portugal.

' I order you, sir,' said Craufurd, 'to do your duty. These men shall be punished.'

The Colonel recovered his sword and stepped back smartly to the front of his regiment, while his two riflemen began to unstrap their knapsacks and prepare for the lash. But Craufurd, who had walked to the other side of the square, suddenly turned round and marched quickly back to the 95th.

'Stop!' he ordered. 'In consequence of the intercession of your Lieutenant-Colonel, I will allow you this much; you shall draw lots and the winner shall escape but one of the two I am determined to make an example of.'

The sergeant-major of the 95th immediately stepped down and picked up two straws from the frost-covered stubble at his feet and offered them to the two men. The one who drew the shorter took the shirt from his back and went over to a tree where his wrists were tied to the outstretched branches. He had been sentenced to a hundred lashes, but when the bugler had counted seventy-five, Craufurd ordered him to be taken down and returned to his company.

That night the men reached a part of the country more wild and desolate than any they had yet seen. It was a dreary wilderness, grim and barren, silent and forsaken. The rain, falling with heavy persistence, had washed the snow and frost from the thin, grey, rocky soil. An atmosphere of even deeper despair seemed to fall upon the winding lines of troops as they marched along beneath the overhanging cliffs. Hour after hour, day after night after day, the men struggled on through the cold, wet wilderness to the sea. 'There was now no endeavour to assist one another after a fall', said Rifleman Harris. 'It was every one for himself and God for us all.' As on the march of the other divisions to Corunna, even the women and children were left to fend for themselves. After a halt beside a turnip field, where the men's hunger was so great that they had insubordinately pushed past Colonel Craufurd to snatch the turnips from the waterlogged ground, Harris heard the screams of a child. He turned round, to see one of the women

> endeavouring to drag along a little boy of about seven or eight years of age. The poor child was apparently completely exhausted, and his legs failing under him. The mother had occasionally, up to this time, been assisted by some of the men, taking it in turns to help the little fellow on; but now all further appeal was vain. No man had more strength than was necessary for the support of his own carcass, and the mother could no longer raise the child in her arms, as her reeling pace too plainly showed. Still, however, she continued to drag the child along with her. It was a pitiable sight, and wonderful to behold the efforts the poor woman made to keep the boy among us. At last the little fellow had not even strength to cry, but, with mouth wide open, stumbled onwards, until both sank down to rise no more.

So tired that they lost all count of time; so hungry that a lump of black bread and a cup of sour wine eaten under the warily suspicious eyes of a peasant in a wayside hovel was a meal to be remembered for ever; so dispirited that they no longer cared if they died, they marched on silently. Often they would hear the clatter and splash of hooves behind them or hear a harsh, familiar voice and look up to see old 'Black Bob' Craufurd scowling down at them with a hint of pity in his stern, dark eyes. Often he would look at them like this, quietly inspecting their faces, not speaking to them. But sometimes he would make a gruffly encouraging remark, and even smile before riding on again to the next company, shouting over his shoulder, 'Keep your ranks there, men! Keep your ranks and move on – *no straggling* from the main body.'

There were those, of course, who could not keep on. They lay in ditches and beneath the bleak shelter of rocks and petrified-looking trees for miles along the rain-washed tracks between Ponferrada and Orense. One man, who had stumbled into a morass during a night march and had exhausted himself in clambering out of it, struggled on to rejoin his regiment over tracks where the dead and dying lay like the grotesque mileposts of a nightmare. One group of 'poor devils were still alive but, both men and women, unable to proceed. They were sitting huddled together in the road, their heads drooping forward and apparently awaiting their end.' Even the dead which he passed 'occasionally lying on the line of march . . . looked comfortless in their last sleep'. At length he caught up with the brigade and found the men 'linked together arm-in-arm like a party of drunkards. They were composed of various regiments; many were bare-headed and without shoes; and some with their heads tied up in old rags and fragments of handkerchiefs.'

And then at last, towards the end of the second week of the retreat, the men reached the top of yet another hill and saw far away below them, through the tears in their bloodshot eyes, the masts of English ships in Vigo harbour. They ran on down to the beach, and the inhabitants ran out to see them and stood aghast at the sight.

'Our beards were long and ragged', one of the survivors wrote. 'Almost all were without shoes and stockings; many had their clothes and accoutrements in fragments, with their heads swathed in old rags, and our weapons were covered with rust; whilst not a few had now, from toil and fatigue, become quite blind.'

11

Betanzos to Corunna

'Whenever we gained the summit of a hill, all eyes were on the watch to catch a glimpse of the long looked out for ships.'

Captain Patterson, 50th Regiment

FROM THE HILLS around Betanzos the rest of the army could also see the sea. For days the men had been thinking about it: whenever they 'gained the summit of a hill,' said Captain Patterson of the 50th, 'all eyes were on the watch to catch a glimpse of the long looked out for ships. One height after another was ascended but still nothing in sight.' But now the ocean was below them and they could just discern in the distance the masts in the bay. An officer with a glass announced to his 'company of scarecrows' that they were flying flags on which he could distinguish the colours of the Royal Navy.

As if to welcome them to the coastal plain, where the orange trees were already in flower and the rye in ear, the clouds were blown away in a gentle breeze and the sun came out. There were wild flowers everywhere, and the country lanes were like the lanes of England. The stores were full of food and although some regiments were ill served by a Commissariat which had now completely collapsed, most of them got as much as they could eat. After they had had their meat the soldiers pushed their naked, frost-bitten feet into the soft, long grass and felt alive again.

On January 11th they formed up before daylight and marched down to the bridge at Burgo across the tidal Mero river. Despite their ragged clothes and filthy unshaven faces they presented a soldier-like appearance, as they marched regiment by regiment across the bridge and through the villages of Piedralonga and Eiris into Corunna. As each battalion passed into the town, Moore rode up to its commanding officer and complimented him or, more often, castigated him for its behaviour during the retreat. Most battalions had lost more than 100 men. The 6th, whose conduct Moore had had occasion to criticise more than once, had lost nearly 400; the 9th had lost over 300; many other regiments had left behind almost as many. Apart from the regiments of the rearguard, only the Guards had preserved their reputation. 'Those must be the Guards',

The brigades under Major-General Fraser crossing the River Tagus near Villa Velha from an aquatint after an eye-witness sketch by the Rev. William Bradford

A snow-covered pass in Galicia from a sketch by Sir Robert Ker Porter

The road to Corunna from a sketch by Sir Robert Ker Porter

Corunna Harbour at the time of the explosion on 13th January 1809 from a sketch by
Sir Robert Ker Porter

View of Corunna during the battle by H. Lecomte

Battle of Corunna, 16 January 1809 from an aquatint by M. Duborg, after a contemporary drawing by W. Heath

The Burial of Sir John Moore

Moore said with satisfaction, as two battalions, each 800 strong, came into view, led by a drum major twirling his staff, their drums tapping rhythmically in the warm and pleasant air. The condition of the army as a whole, however, so dismayed some of Moore's senior officers that they suggested to him it was his duty to ask Soult for an armistice rather than fight a battle which they could not hope to win. Moore immediately rejected the suggestion, and rode away to reconnoitre the ground which he was determined to defend.

When all the divisions had crossed the bridge at Burgo, General Edward Paget was left with the reserve to perform the last duty of the rearguard and keep the French on the eastern side of the river while arrangements were made for the embarkation of the army. Elaborate measures had been taken by the engineers to blow Burgo bridge, as in almost every case since they had destroyed the stone bridge over the Esla at Castro Gonzalo they had failed in their endeavours to blow up another one.

'What, sir!' General Paget had exclaimed only the day before to an engineer officer whose charge had exploded in an impressive roar and cloud of smoke but had left the bridge at Betanzos intact. 'What, another abortion! And pray, sir, how do you account for this failure?'

The engineer could not account for it to General Paget's satisfaction, but he was determined to have more success at Burgo. He placed enough barrels of gunpowder beneath the arches to blow up a bridge four times its size. The officers of the light company of the 28th, however, taking it as a matter of course that it would be another affair of sound and smoke, took their men over the bridge after the rest of the reserve division had crossed and drew them up close behind it on the northern bank. Seeing the size and number of the charges some of the men remonstrated against their nearness, but they were assured that they were more than safe. After a long wait, while the engineer carefully checked his fuses and trains, the charge was at last ignited. The air was suddenly rent by an explosion of such resounding force that it was heard by a midshipman in Corunna harbour. 'Large blocks of masonry whizzed awfully over our heads', said an officer of the 28th,

> and caused what the whole of Soult's cavalry could not effect during the retreat. The light company of the 28th and Captain Cameron's company of the 95th broke their ranks and ran like turkeys, and regardless of their bodies crammed their heads into any hole which promised security.

Not all of them found security. As the great hunks of masonry hurtled through the air and, falling heavily to the earth, buried themselves deeply in the ground, one man was killed by a rock which almost cut him in two, and another four were so severely wounded that they had to be carried back into Corunna.

But the bridge was destroyed; and that evening the 28th and the 95th were able to look back across the river at the French cavalry patrols, who came up to the eastern bank just before nightfall, with a stronger sense of safety than they had been able to feel for days. The advanced companies occupied houses in the village of Burgo, with outposts and sentries by the rubble of the bridge and along the banks of the river.

On the morning of the 12th, enemy infantry came up to the river and for two days the reserve division and Soult's leading regiments fired at each other across the Mero. The reserve were kept supplied with enormous quantities of ammunition from Corunna, while the ammunition of the French which had been carried for hundreds of miles across the mountains had to be used with more caution.

Food was as plentiful in the reserve division as ammunition. Potatoes, which the men had not seen since they had left Salamanca, had been brought ashore by the ton from the fleet, and four-pound pieces of salt pork were as commonplace as cartridges. Many of the men were able to vary their diet with chicken for the capture of which they had perfected an unusual technique. Lying on the ground they cackled and clucked so realistically that the birds obediently trooped out towards the soldiers' hiding place and were seized and strangled in the midst of their first terror-stricken squawks.

Some officers of the 28th, having prepared what Ensign Blakeney declared was 'a sumptuous dinner', invited their friend Captain Cameron of the 95th to share it with them. The house which they occupied was under constant small arms fire but there was one corner of a ground-floor room in which their guest could feel as secure as in a London coffee-house. By holding out a cap on the point of a sword they drew the French fire on to one side of the house, while Cameron dashed across the street to the other, suffering no worse injury than a bullet through the tail of his greatcoat. He crawled across the floor to the table and sat down to enjoy his meal while a soldier acted as butler by creeping along the floor, pushing the dishes before him and standing up to serve them when he reached the safe corner of the room. The only disturbance came when Lieutenant Hill of the 28th placed his wine glass beyond the safety line drawn across the table to see it immediately shattered by a musket ball.

The young officers arranged to meet the following evening for another meal, but the appointment could not be kept. On January 13th Franceski's cavalry found a bridge downstream at Cela, which the engineers had not destroyed, and crossed the Mero in force. Moore ordered Paget to withdraw the reserve division from Burgo before he was cut off. As dusk fell the men withdrew up the river road towards Corunna. When they reached the town they heard for the first time that the ships they had seen from the heights beyond the river were only hospital and store ships. The transports which the General had ordered were still beating about in the Atlantic having failed to double Cape Finisterre. No one knew when they would arrive. For the moment the army was stranded in Corunna and might now have to fight a battle with its back against the sea.

PART FOUR

Corunna

12

Harbour

'The danger is now unequivocally perceived, and people begin to meet it manfully.'

Mr. Henry Crabb Robinson

THE PEOPLE OF CORUNNA seemed to the soldiers to be more industrious, more patriotic, more hospitable than any other people they had come across in Spain. 'They expressed a fixed determination', wrote a commissary, 'to be buried under the ruins of their ramparts rather than submit to the enemy . . . . Had the Spaniards been as patriotic everywhere else, things would have gone better, and we might possibly have still been standing ground at Salamanca.' The troops had become used to indifference or to absurd confidence and vain promises, but in Corunna there were signs that the promises would be fulfilled. Men and women, 'troops of young and beautiful girls', even children went in procession up to the front with baskets of ammunition on their heads and cases of cartridges in their arms and, despite the punishments which they expected subsequently to endure, cheerfully helped in dismantling the sea forts. The mayor, on a fine Andalusian stallion, galloped round the streets, shouting words of encouragement and giving advice. Shopkeepers and barbers were given muskets from the British stores and looked as if they meant to use them, copying the British soldiers who, in a naval officer's phrase, tossed them about 'with the air of veteran sportsmen eager to try their new pieces'. 'The danger is now unequivocally perceived,' *The Times* correspondent wrote, 'and people begin to meet it manfully.' Even the theatre was closed, and the players went to work on the ramparts.

The sense of danger and urgency was given a fearful emphasis on the morning of January 13th when the artillery had completed their arrangements to blow up 1,500 barrels of gunpowder which had been sent out from England many months before and had not been used. A cavalry officer was taking a detachment of men to collect some straw from a magazine when the earth suddenly rocked beneath his feet as if an earthquake had taken place. Another explosion soon followed, more terrible and alarming in its effects than the first. The earth seemed to rock to and fro, houses tottered, windows and loose fragments strewed the streets, horror and consternation, in fact, were depicted upon the countenance of all. Those out of doors prostrated themselves in the streets; while the shrieks and moans of those inside were appalling.

Captain Gordon, who was having breakfast, thought that the enemy had begun a bombardment of the town and that a shell had fallen on the house. Outside in the streets hundreds of people, many of them half-dressed or in their night clothes, knelt in prayer amidst the fragments of glass from the shattered *miradores,* 'repeating their "Aves" with an energy proportioned to their fright'. In the harbour the ships rocked as if tossed by a violent storm, and a tidal wave rolled across the walls of the quay. While above the ruins of the powder store two immense columns of black smoke and dust soared up to a great height, as a shower of broken masonry fell to the earth with a roaring sound and killed several people who had been caught in the open.

The sky was bright and the air perfectly calm, so that the thick black columns remained stationary for a long time before they curled away over the sea. An officer of the 15th Hussars, who ran over to find out what had caused so vast an explosion, was told that the artillery officer in charge of the operation had not discovered that the building containing the 1,500 barrels of powder adjoined another one where there were nearly 5,000 more.

Other stores were less thoroughly destroyed. Most of the artillery wagons that had escaped the holocaust at Villafranca were thrown over the cliffs into the sea, but several more found their way into the sheds of farmers in exchange for a cask or two of wine. Spare muskets were also afterwards discovered by the French in the villages south of the town. A storehouse containing cavalry swords was raided by a gang of boys who spent hours marching up and down the streets with the heavy, naked blades resting on their shoulders. And a consignment of clothes sent out from England as a gift to the Spanish armies was left on the quayside by a supercargo who could not bring himself either to take them back or to throw them into the water.

By January 14th, however, most of what could not be used by the British army and its Spanish assistants had been destroyed. On the evening of that day over 100 transports sailed into the bay from Vigo, escorted by twelve warships, and at last the embarkation could begin. Hastily, before the wind should change, the remainder of the sick, all the guns except nine, and all the cavalry regiments, which would be of little use on the rocky broken slopes outside the town, were sent aboard. Less than 1,000 horses went with them. The rest had to be killed.

Men who had become inured to the sufferings and death of their fellows broke down and cried unashamedly as they watched the animals die; for the slaughter was performed with appalling clumsiness. The horses were brought to the edge of the cliffs overhanging the beach and were shot and then pushed over on to the sands below where soldiers with hammers 'despatched those who had landed there alive because of a badly aimed shot'. So uncertainly, in fact, were the pistols aimed that the men were advised to cut the horses' throats with swords instead of trying to shoot them. Many terrified horses neighed and screamed at the sight of their fellows struggling on the blood-splashed beach, and breaking loose they galloped down the cliffs and along the sea-shore, with their manes erect and their mouths wide open. Soon the streets of the town were filled with frightened and wounded horses pushing with their forefeet at the rubbish heaps and the cabbage leaves and refuse in the open drains. One of them, belonging to an officer in the 18th Light Dragoons who had gone aboard the fleet, tried frantically to reach his master and twice swam out to the ship in the vain hope of joining him.

Before morning the last cavalry man was aboard, but Moore could not hope that the infantry would be able to follow them with as little interference from the enemy. Reports had reached him that Soult's engineers had come up to repair the bridge at Burgo a few hours after Paget had been withdrawn, and the infantry divisions of Merle and Mermet were now streaming across it towards the Heights of Palavea and Penasquedo, only three miles south of the town. Moore had considered occupying these hills himself. They rose to a height of about 600 feet, whereas the ridge of Monte Mero, which ran parallel to them nearer the town and on which he had decided to place his army, had an extreme height of only 400 feet. But the Palavea and Penasquedo Heights were too extensive for him to hold with his depleted army, and he felt compelled to make the most of the mile-and-a-half-long Monte Mero which was both dominated and outflanked by them. By occupying this relatively narrow ridge he was, of course, running the danger of having his flank turned. But he hoped that by a careful disposition of his 15,000 infantry and nine guns he might be able to turn the apparent weakness of his position to advantage.

Towards the western end of the Monte Mero, the fall of the slope into the valley is broken by a low ridge of land which runs across the valley towards the opposing hills. On this low neck of land stood the little village of Elvina, a group of scattered lime-washed houses, with brown pan-tiled roofs and gardens enclosed by dry stone walls, surrounding a small church

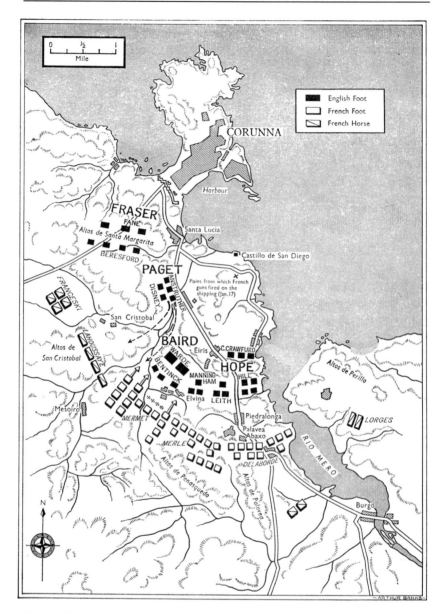

The Battle of Corunna

with an open belfry. Here it was that Moore could expect an attack. Further east the slope fell more steeply to the valley, and, although Soult might try to advance against this more difficult left flank, by pushing up the road from Burgo through the little hamlets of Palavea Abaxo and Piedralonga, he would not be able to outflank it for its far end rested on the cliffs above the estuary.

It was then against his centre and right that Moore hoped Soult would make his attack. If he did so, Moore was ready for him. On the crest of Monte Mero he placed only two of his four divisions; the other two he held back in reserve, Paget's at Eiris and Fraser's in the suburb of Santa Lucia on the southern outskirts of Corunna. Hope's division – with Hill's brigade on the far left by the sea, Leith's beside it on the landward side of the Burgo to Corunna road, and with Catlin Crawfurd's brigade in reserve – he placed on the seaward flank of the ridge. In the centre and on the right he put Baird's division, with Manningham's brigade next to Leith's, Warde's Guards brigade behind it in reserve; and on the far right, looking down on Elvina and across the west towards the Heights of San Cristobal, the brigade of Lord William Bentinck who had rejoined the army from his diplomatic appointment in Madrid. Bentinck's brigade comprised the 4th Regiment, the 42nd Royal Highland Regiment and the 50th. It was these three regiments which would bear the brunt of the initial assault if Soult attacked in the way that Moore expected.

Should the French succeed in driving through them, or try to outflank them by advancing up the valley between Monte Mero and the Heights of San Cristobal, Moore could bring Paget's reserve division round from Eiris and thus extend his right. If, on the other hand, Soult tried to break through his left, Paget could be sent forward to reinforce Hope. In any eventuality Fraser's division would not be immediately engaged and could be brought forward from the Corunna suburbs and used as it was needed.

Three of his guns he gave to Paget; the remaining six he placed in pairs along the crest of Monte Mero. When daylight came on January 15th these guns had been waiting silently for four days. Moore had begun to doubt that the French would attack at all.

Marshal Soult from the Heights of Penasquedo could see the English lining the ridge of Monte Mero across the valley in front of him, and he could see too, beneath the western edge of the ridge, the inviting ground which led straight into Corunna. He had made up his mind to attack and he had decided to do it in the way that Moore had hoped. He planned to contain the English left and centre, attack their right and push a combined force of cavalry and infantry past their right flank beneath the western end of Monte Mero. When the attack against the right flank was well advanced he would press hard against the centre and left, to prevent the troops here going back to the assistance of the retreating wing.

During the morning of January 15th, when Delaborde's division had crossed the Mero river, the men of Mermet's and Merle's divisions came up to the crest of the Penasquedo Heights. On their right Delaborde's division climbed up the Heights of Palavea and dragged up two guns which before noon were firing across the valley at the forward regiments of Hope's division. Colonel M'Kenzie of the 5th decided to take some companies of his regiment through the village of Piedralonga and make a charge on the guns which, so far as he could see, were unsupported. He led his men through the village and then opened them up in line for the charge up the slope beyond it. They ran a few yards only. Suddenly, from behind a curving, low stone wall beneath the guns, a line of French infantry rose up and fired a volley of devastating effect. Colonel M'Kenzie and several of his men dropped dead. The rest turned and fled down the slope.

On the right, also, some lives were lost as a force of French cavalry edged forward and began a skirmish in the valley beneath the Heights of San Cristobal which continued intermittently all day. By nightfall each side had lost about 100 men.

Soult by now was able to spare them. His three infantry divisions comprised thirty-nine battalions of about 500 men each and he had also under command by this time three cavalry divisions, those of Franceski, Lahoussaye and Lorges. His total force numbered rather more than 16,000 men. He had, in addition, forty guns and when darkness had fallen he gave orders for those not already supporting Delaborde's division on the Heights of Palavea to be dragged up the rocky Heights of Penasquedo, where most of them were to be placed in battery facing the right of the English line above the village of Elvina. The operation of manhandling the heavy guns up the steep slopes of the Penasquedo Heights, through wide tracts of gorse and over slippery ground broken by narrow ravines and enormous granite boulders, was one of extreme difficulty. But before dawn the guns were in position, and the infantry around them ready to attack.

Moore was asleep in a house on the Canton Grande. After an exhausting day spent mostly in the saddle, he had gone to bed late after writing his last despatch and had been woken from a sound sleep between two and three o'clock in the morning by his Military Secretary who had an important report to hand to him.

'It's Colborne, sir', the Military Secretary said and was obliged to repeat the words more than once before Sir John stirred in his sleep. But, when he did so and sat up in bed, he was immediately fully awake and asked Colborne many questions before sending him away to eat the meal which François, Moore's faithful French servant, had kept for him.

'Now, if there is no bungling,' Moore said as Colborne left the room, 'I don't see why we should not all be off safely to-morrow.'

13

The Battle: Morning and Afternoon

'Thrown on its haunches the animal came, sliding and dashing the dirt up
with its fore feet, thus bending the General forward almost to its neck; but
his head was thrown back and his look more keenly piercing than I ever
saw it.'

Major Charles Napier, 50th Regiment

THREE HOURS LATER the General was on his feet again. It was six o'clock
in the morning of 16th January 1809. A mist had come up from the sea
and swirled across the harbour walls and down the valleys between the
silent hills. Moore mounted his large cream and black horse and rode off
to his forward outposts along the ridge of Monte Mero. Colonel Graham
was with him and Colonel Robert Long who had sailed up from Vigo
to join the Headquarters staff two days before. It was a cold morning and
the ground was hard underfoot.

The outposts were quiet. Little had been heard during the night from
across the valley, and as the sun rose over the crest of the Heights of Perillo
the French troops remained motionless in their positions to the south.
The air was clear and bright and it was possible to see the French positions
quite distinctly. A naval officer noticed how the soldiers looked at them
and then over their shoulders wistfully towards the sea.

At ten o'clock Moore was back in the town watching the tenders
moving busily about between the ships in the bay and the piles of baggage
on the quayside. In a few more hours now, if the French made no move,
the army would be away. He told Colonel Anderson, who had been
acting as Adjutant-General since Brigadier-General Clinton had gone to
bed with dysentery, that he hoped all the remaining baggage and horses
would be aboard by four o'clock as he wanted the boats to be free by
then for the embarkation of the reserve division. 'Remember,' he said to
him, 'remember, I depend upon your paying particular attention to
everything that concerns the embarkation. Let there be as little confusion
as possible.'

At twelve o'clock the men of the reserve received orders to march for
the harbour. After an early dinner they filed down through the town

towards the transports. They had just been told that, as they had distinguished themselves during the retreat, they would be rewarded by being sent on board ship first and thus be given the opportunity of appropriating the most comfortable places. They were in good humour, well fed and contented. Their minds were occupied, one of them remembered, 'by thoughts of home'. Mr. Robinson passed them on his way back to the hotel where he had his midday meal. He had spent the morning in paying farewell visits in the town and in writing his last letter to *The Times*. At the hotel he found the dining-room filled with English officers eating what they hoped would be their last Spanish meal. Outside the windows more English soldiers marched past and the waiters watched them silently 'in a sort of gloomy anger'.

Suddenly the whole scene changed. Robinson looked up from his dinner and found the whole room empty – 'not a red coat to be seen'. People rushed up to roofs and balconies, and sailors clambered up the ships' rigging looking inland towards the hills. An aide-de-camp went galloping down the town towards the troops waiting by the water's edge. They had already heard the sound of gun-fire in the south and were looking at each other 'with anxious enquiry'. They were not kept long in suspense. The aide-de-camp reined up by their colonel and ordered them back to the front.

Moore was already there. A few minutes before he had received a report from General Hope: 'The enemy's lines are getting under arms.' He had immediately struck spurs into his horse and galloped towards his forward divisions. His expression was astonishingly transformed. The day before an officer in the engineers had seen him looking 'wistfully at the enemy, apparently wishing with painful eagerness for a battle'. Now his wish had been fulfilled. Thomas Graham could scarcely have 'believed it possible for a man so worn down with fatigue and anxiety to have been so transformed. It was a transition from fixed gloom bordering almost on despair, to a state of exaltation.' Moore's face was almost boyish in its gaiety.

Already the advanced picquets on the right of the British line were beginning to fall back before a surging, irregular mass of 600 French light troops pouring down into the valley from the Heights of Penasquedo. They were led by General Jardon, a tough, scarcely literate old soldier, hard-drinking and hard-swearing, who dispensed with aides-de-camp and horses and marched with his men, a musket in his hand and a dirty shirt on his back. Behind his *tirailleurs,* already visible on the skyline in the regular, intimidating columns that had overawed an entire continent, came the main body of General Mermet's infantry. And on the hills beyond them the heavy French guns roared and smoked, sending salvoes of round-shot over their heads and into the waiting ranks of the British troops drawn up on the opposing heights.

As the French infantry stumbled down the steep slope towards the village of Elvina, eight regiments of French cavalry under Lahoussaye and Franceski trotted out from the cover of the hills behind them and edged northwards along the lower slopes of the San Cristobal hills, as if to get round the right of the British front-line troops and cut them off from their line of retreat to Corunna. Moore saw these movements and immediately understood them. To check the turning movements of the cavalry on his right he sent back orders to Fraser to move out of the Corunna suburbs on to the heights of Santa Margarita, and orders to Paget to move westwards from Eiris towards San Cristobal. Then he galloped off to deal personally with the infantry attack in his front.

He found, as he had expected, that the main force of the enemy assault was directed against Lord William Bentinck's brigade on the extreme right of his line. Further to his left, parties of skirmishers moved down into the valley to exchange shots with the picquets of his three other brigades nearer the sea; and behind these skirmishers a column of enemy infantry was already pushing General Hope's outposts out of the village of Palavea. But the attack here seemed no more than a diversion and Moore concentrated on the danger to his right where Mermet's heavy columns of French infantry were moving with such determination behind Jardon's dense swarms of *tirailleurs*. Now walking, now running, they came on shouting, '*En avant! Tuez! Tuez! Tuez! En avant!*', pushing the English picquets before them, driving the light company of the 59th Regiment out of the village and then advancing up the slopes of Monte Mero.

Major Charles Napier, commanding the 50th, was peering shortsightedly down into the valley at the advancing *tirailleurs,* when he heard the sound of galloping hooves behind him and turned round in his saddle to see a horse and rider appear so suddenly at his back that they 'seemed to have alighted from the air'. Both man and horse, Napier wrote afterwards, looked at

the approaching foe with an intenseness that seemed to concentrate all feeling in their eyes. The sudden stop of the animal, a cream-coloured one with black tail and mane, had cast the latter streaming forward, its ears were pushed out like horns, while its eyes flashed fire, and it snorted loudly with expanded nostrils, expressing terror, astonishment and muscular exertion. My first thought was, it will be away like the wind! But then I looked at the rider and the horse was forgotten. Thrown on its haunches the animal came, sliding and dashing the dirt up with its fore feet, thus bending the general forward almost to its neck; but his head was thrown back and his look more keenly piercing than I ever before saw it. He glanced to the right and left, and then fixed his eyes intently on the enemy's advancing column, at the same time grasping the reins with both hands, and pressing the horse firmly with his knees: his body thus seemed to deal with the animal while his mind was intent on the enemy, and his aspect was one of searching intenseness beyond the power of words to describe: for a while he looked, and then galloped to the left, without uttering a word.

Encouraged by this inspiring vision Major Napier rode across his front to the right of his regiment where the fire seemed strongest, to share the dangers of his men. He noticed that each time a cannon shot whistled over their heads they all ducked. 'Don't duck', he told them cheerfully. 'The ball has passed before you hear the whizz.' But the instinct was irresistible. Only one man was able to restrain himself. He was uncommonly short and, as his neighbours continued to bob their heads compulsively above him, he maintained a rigid composure as he looked calmly down the slope at the advancing enemy.

'You are a little fellow,' Major Napier called to him, 'but the tallest man in the 50th to-day for all that – come to me after the battle and you shall be a sergeant.'

And then Napier turned his horse's head to ride back along his line. He never saw the little man again.

As he rode back towards his left he passed one of his company commanders, Charles Stanhope, standing in front of his men, brave and stolid, while the balls cut through the air just over his head. He was so tall that Napier thought he would surely be hit if he stayed where he was and ordered him to move back into a hollow.

The men of his left flank companies were falling fast, hit by musket balls and crushed by the hurtling weight of the round-shot that skimmed the crest of the ridge and bounced across the turf. Napier knew he could not keep them in so exposed a position much longer and began to wonder what to do. He had been given no orders. His brigadier, Bentinck, was nowhere to be seen. Baird, the divisional commander, had already been badly wounded by a round-shot which had all but wrenched his left arm off at the shoulder and had been carried off the field. And then Napier saw Moore again. Could he, he asked him, send down his grenadier company into the enclosures in front. The company was losing men fast and the French *tirailleurs* were getting dangerously close.

'No,' Moore said, 'they will fire on our picquets in the village.'

' Sir,' Napier protested, 'our picquets, and those of the 4th also, were driven from thence when you went to the left.'

'Were they? Then you are right. Send out your grenadiers.'

As soon as he had given the order, Moore galloped off again as quickly as he had come.

'Clunes!' Napier shouted to the enormously tall captain in command of the grenadier company. 'Take your grenadiers and open the ball.'

As the grenadiers moved off, the General once more appeared with that same startling effect of an apparition that Napier was long afterwards to remember so vividly. At the moment of his joining Napier a round-shot struck the ground between their horses' feet. Moore's horse leaped round but neither horse nor rider was hurt. A man of the 42nd, however, standing nearby had his leg torn off and falling to the ground rolled and screamed in agony. So horrible were his screams that the men on either side of him edged away from him, looking in horror at his convulsions and the blood pouring from his stump.

'This is nothing, my lads', the General said sharply, pulling the men together again by the firm authority of his voice. 'Take that man away. My good fellow, don't make such a noise. We must bear these things better.'

The ranks closed over the blood-splashed ground and Moore rode off again. He had satisfied himself by now that the attacks on his centre and left were certainly, as he had at first supposed, attempts to divert his attention from Soult's endeavour to turn his right. He was ready to counter-attack and was watching for the most favourable opportunity with an excitement which, as Colonel Graham saw, was almost ecstatic in its intensity. He must not attack too soon. His back was to the sea and an error might be fatal. His troops were well placed to combat the French design but they must be handled carefully and well. He saw the French cavalry were having difficulty in picking their way over the broken ground and between the dry stone walls in the valley to his right, and could safely hope that Fraser and Paget would soon be in position to check their advance. He saw too a brigade of infantry from Mermet's division take the same route round his flank and he let them come on as well. But, as soon as they were within musket range, he sent an order to Colonel Wynch, commanding the 4th on his extreme right, telling him to draw back his outstretched wing to form a right angle with the rest, so that half the men could fire down the slope to the west while the others still watched their front. He watched the movement carried out. It was done perfectly. The men on the far right backed away, firing as they moved, as calmly and smoothly as if they had been on parade. 'That is exactly how it should be done', Moore called to them, and the officers of the 4th remembered his words with pride.

Turning to the slopes in front, where the leading *tirailleurs* were now not much more than fifty yards below him, Moore saw at last his opportunity. After passing Elvina, the French 31st Regiment had split into two. And having done so, the right-hand column, which had been marching up the slope against the 42nd Regiment, halted to deploy. This was his chance. He ordered the 42nd to charge. A few moments later Colonel Sterling was leading his tall Highlanders down towards the enemy. They fired a well-aimed volley and then rushed on with the bayonet. There was a burst of ferocious shouting, a brief and savage struggle, and then the French gave ground. They soon recovered, however, and the Highlanders were held half-way down the slope.

Above them Major Napier was still without orders. His brigadier had ambled up to him on a mule, 'and began talking', Napier said, 'as if we were going to have breakfast'. But he brought no orders and Napier was so agitated that he could not bring himself to listen to what Lord William Bentinck was saying in his slow, even-tempered voice. With his eyes on the approaching French and the conversational tone of Lord William's friendly words in his ears, he thought to himself, 'That chap takes it coolly or the devil's in it!' When his brigadier rode unconcernedly off towards the 4th Regiment, Major Napier turned back anxiously to his own. His men were becoming restless and uneasy and several gaps had formed in his line. He walked up and down in front of it, making the men shoulder and order arms continually as the only thing he could think of to occupy their minds. The colours of the regiment had become a mark for the enemy's guns on the ridge opposite, so he ordered them to be lowered before the men around them were destroyed. Still no orders came for him.

'Good God, Montgomery,' he said in exasperation to an old officer who had been commissioned from the ranks, 'are we not to advance?'

'I think we ought.'

'But no orders have come.'

'I would not wait.'

Many Highlanders lay dead and wounded on the slope below him. The others, crouched behind the low stone walls of the enclosures, seemed too few to resist another French assault.

'You cannot be wrong to follow the 42nd', Montgomery pressed him, and so Napier decided to act.

He gave his men the order to advance. Not feeling at all confident that he should be moving forward without authority, he forbade the men to open fire so that he would be able to keep them in control and withdraw them to the higher ground if he were to be recalled. They marched down towards the 42nd, still performing their arms drill, taking their muskets up to the slope and then down to the carry position with relentless formality.

'Major, let us fire', many of them called out to Napier. But he would not let them. 'Not yet', he kept calling back. 'Not yet.'

They came up against some Highlanders of the 42nd held up behind one of the walls that straggled irregularly across the slopes, like the broken and petrified skeletons of immense beasts, and for a moment they too rested there. 'Forward! Forward!' a Highland officer was shouting but for the moment the 42nd could not be moved. The men of the 50th stepped across their backs and over the wall towards the French troops beyond it.

'Do you see your enemies plain enough to hit them now?' Napier asked, his own weak eyes peering through the smoke.

'By Jasus we do', several Irish voices replied.

'Then blaze away!'

In a crackling torrent of sound the advance continued until another stone wall halted it again. The men came up to the wall and knelt behind it, waiting for an officer to lead them over. Major Stanhope came up and leapt over the wall and about 100 men followed him. But the others stayed where they were. Snatching a pike from one of his sergeants, Napier dived at their backs. Cursing and shouting, wielding the pike with furious energy, he pushed and prodded and knocked the men over the wall and then led them charging down after Stanhope. Going back for more men with Sergeant Keene, Napier almost had his head blown off by those who still stood firing their muskets on the safe side of the wall. Keene managed just in time to push the barrels of the muskets aside with his pike, but his face and Napier's were both badly burned by the flames from the powder.

In a disordered mass the 50th rushed on down the slope, followed now by groups of Highlanders, and closed in on Elvina. The French fell back before them, firing well and bringing many of the wild attackers tumbling to the ground. At the head of the excited British troops, Napier in his cocked hat and the lanky figure of Stanhope could clearly be seen from the crest of the ridge above.

'Well done, my Majors!' Moore called out in admiration as he watched them running down towards the village under a heavy fire.

Close behind them two ensigns carried the regiment's colours as a rallying point in the smoke, and when they fell the colours were picked up by two sergeants, who took them down into the marshy ground at the bottom of the valley. The fire was heavier than ever here. Napier's sword belt was shot from his waist as men stumbled to the ground, screaming with pain, all round him.

On every side French soldiers too lay on the ground, their faces buried in the reeds and grass.

'Bayonet them!' the British troops shouted, close to hysteria. 'Bayonet them! They're pretending.'

'No', Napier shouted back. 'No. Leave the cowards. There are plenty who bear arms to kill. Come on! Come on!'

He led them on again, into the village and past the church and saw beyond the church a lane running up beside a rocky mound. At the top of the lane, the French columns were reforming. Shouting to his men to follow, he dashed up the lane to press home the attack while the enemy were still disorganised. But most of his men had gone as far as they dared. They had found some sheltering rocks around the church, and had decided it would be a better plan to wait there and keep up a fire on the French until reinforcements came.

Only three officers and thirty men followed Napier up the lane, and before they had gone many paces several of these few were killed. As well as musket-fire there was grape-shot to contend with now, and scores of shells burst in the air and amongst the rocks, sending jagged bits of iron flying and whining through the smoke. The explosions cracked in Napier's ears and made them ring wildly. He felt almost out of his mind. Half-way up the lane he fell, without knowing why; and he heard through the high-pitched din in his ears, a soldier's voice cry out, 'The Major's killed'.

'Not yet', he called back. 'Come on!'

At the top of the lane there was a breastwork of loose stones which a forward picquet of the 4th had made the day before, and Napier led his men breathlessly towards it. Twelve of them reached it. But there was no peace for them there either. Three or four men were killed at Napier's side as they squatted panting behind the barrier and two others were shot in the back by men of their own regiment firing from the village behind them.

'Oh, God! Major,' one of them said, 'our own men are killing us! Oh, Christ God! I'm shot in the back of the head.' He fell against Napier who saw the hole in his head just above the tightly drawn hairs of his pig-tail. Napier remembered that his father had once told him how he had saved a man's life at the siege of Charleston by pulling a ball out of a man's head with his fingers before inflammation swelled the wound around it. Napier put his finger in but he could not find the ball. He felt sick and dared not press too far in for fear of crushing the brain. The man died in his arms and the misery of it all made Napier 'so wild as to cry and stamp with rage, feeling a sort of despair at seeing the soldiers did not come on'.

He sent back the three officers with a sergeant who had also reached the wall unscathed, and told them to force the men to come on. The French battery which was firing on them was not far beyond the far side of the wall and he thought with a few more men he could charge and overthrow it. But he must have more men. There were only three left with him now. The officers and sergeant ran back and found Major Stanhope near the church, wondering what to do. 'Good God!' Stanhope called out when he saw them. 'Where is Napier?'

They told him and he shouted at the men around him to follow him up the lane. A few moved from behind the rocks, but Stanhope had taken only a few steps when he slumped to the ground, shot through the heart. And shout and swear as they did, the other officers could not get a man to move out into the murderous fire to follow Stanhope's example. In despair they ran back to Napier.

When he heard that his men could not be moved and that his friend Stanhope was dead, Napier lost control of himself. He jumped to the top of the breastwork and turning his back on the enemy he waved his cocked hat and sword frantically above his head and called at the top of his voice to the men behind him to come on. But his shouts were lost in the roar of battle and his gestures half-hidden by the smoke. He stood shouting and waving for several seconds in his blood-soaked uniform, but his men could not hear him and they would not move. Those who had followed him to the wall called to him to jump down or he would be killed. 'I thought so too,' he confessed, 'but was so mad as to care little what happened to me.' In fact not a shot was fired at him. For a French captain, overcome with admiration and pity, forbade his men to shoot and other French officers did the same.

If his own men would not follow him, Napier decided, he would try to collect some others from the 42nd. 'Stay here as long as you can', he said to Captain Harrison, the senior of the three officers who had come with him to the wall. 'I will go to the left and try to make out how the 42nd get on.'

There was a lane to the left, running along the crest of a little ridge with a high hedge on the enemy side of it. He decided to make a dash for this lane and run along in the shadow of the hedge until he found out where the 42nd were. If he could get together thirty men, he thought, he would have enough to overrun the battery. He ran off towards the lane, his uniform, face and hands covered with blood, armed only with a short sabre.

He had been running down the lane for some time without seeing anything of either the 42nd or the French when suddenly he almost fell over a wounded French officer lying in the ditch. The officer thought the wild-looking, blood-soaked Englishman was going to kill him and, calling out in alarm, he pointed at Napier with a quick, convulsive movement which brought a blaze of musket fire through the roots of the hedge above him. The balls flying without warning over Napier's head so frightened him that for the first time that day he felt tempted to turn his back and run for his life. But he knew that his own men must be watching him and pulled himself together before he gave way to his immediate impulse. He walked back at a leisurely pace towards the wall where he had left Captain Harrison and his few companions.

They had gone. The only figures in the lane were the crumpled bodies of the dead and the wounded. He turned back down the hill, suddenly conscious of a deep depression. He was stopped by a weak but excited Irish voice.

'Oh! Praised be God! My dear Major! God help you, my darling.'

'I cannot carry you', Napier said. 'Can you walk with my help?'

'Oh no, Major. I am too badly wounded.'

'You must lie there then till help can be found.'

'Oh! Christ God! My jewel, my own dear darling Major. Sure you won't leave me.'

And then the man began to scream in pain and hysteria and terror, and Napier infected by the man's fear became frightened again too. Behind him the French were once more pouring down into Elvina. He stopped to pick the soldier up, but as he did so a musket ball hit him in the leg and smashed the small bone above his ankle. He felt an immediate and exquisite pain and limped away from the man, worrying even then, through the agony of his ankle and the pitiful and alarming screaming, that he had lost the battle for his beloved General.

French troops had re-taken the village.

14

The Battle: Evening

'You can be of no service to me. Go to the soldiers to whom you may be useful.'

Sir John Moore

THE SMOKE HUNG thick in the valley and already the light was beginning to fail. Contradictory and misleading reports had been coming to Moore for an hour, and it was difficult, looking across the partly hidden, broken ground in that uncertain light, to comprehend the opportunities and dangers of the army. It was certain, at least, that the charge of the 50th had been triumphant. Charles Napier had driven the French out of Elvina and up the slopes beyond it by the sheer impetuosity of his assault; and, although his regiment was broken now and the 42nd had also been badly mauled, the enemy having taken the village again were moving up from it for the second time with obvious caution. Moore decided to bring up the brigade of Guards for another frontal assault before the French could fully recover, and he sent Hardinge with a request to Warde to 'fetch them up immediately'. While waiting for their arrival he rode over to the west to see what he could discover of Paget's measures to check the movements of the eight regiments of French cavalry and the five battalions of their infantry round his right flank.

Paget had sent out the 95th in extended order as soon as he had received Moore's first order. A little later the 52nd, with the 28th in support, had joined the 95th and, followed by the other two battalions of the division – the 20th and the 91st – moved along the right bank of the Menelos river. All five battalions moved quickly and had reached the edge of Monte Mero while the enemy cavalry were still stumbling through the maze of rough stone walls and rutted enclosures between the villages of Elvina and San Cristobal in the valley below. Paget lost no time. Within minutes of their arrival on the crest of Monte Mero the 95th were advancing down its western declivities against the French cavalry in that loose, irregular formation which constant practice had perfected.

Unable to charge or even to change front on that broken ground, the French horsemen slowly gave way until Lahoussaye, waving above his head the sword which Napoleon himself had given him, ordered them to dismount and fight as *tirailleurs*. They ranged themselves along the lower slopes of the San Cristobal Heights and opened a sporadic fire. But they were no match for their well-trained enemies. The 95th came on, taking full advantage of the ground, supported by the 28th and 91st, while on their left the 20th and 52nd advanced in line against the infantry who were already under heavy fire from Colonel Wynch's 4th Regiment on the hills above them. It was a model assault in the modern manner. The French, outmanoeuvred by the most skilful light infantry in the world, were forced back towards the Heights of Penasquedo round which they had poured so confidently less than two hours before. They left behind them many prisoners and scores of dead and dying on the slopes.

As they withdrew towards the battery on the crest of the Penasquedo Heights, Moore was planning another attack on that battery from his front. As soon as the Guards arrived, he told his staff, he would send one battalion down to attack a large house and garden on the outskirts of Elvina from which a company of *voltigeurs* was maintaining a fierce fire on the 42nd, who were unable to reply to it because their ammunition was almost finished. The Highlanders, indeed, were growing restless and kept looking over their shoulders for signs of relief or at least an order to replenish their ammunition; and when they saw the Guards marching slowly in their direction they decided to fall back. Moore checked the movement himself. Riding up towards them, he stood up in his stirrups and in a loud voice called to them, 'My brave 42nd, if you've fired your ammunition, you've still your bayonets. Remember Egypt! Think on Scotland! Come on my gallant countrymen.'

Immediately the Highlanders turned about again and went back to face the enemy. Moore raised his hat to them in acknowledgment of their obedience and rode up the hill to the group of staff officers on the crest. He was sitting there watching the 42nd with Colonel Graham, Henry Percy and Captain John Woodford, when Hardinge galloped up to report the Guards' arrival. Moore looked in the direction in which Hardinge was pointing and was suddenly thrown from his saddle. He fell on his back at the feet of Colonel Graham's horse and when Graham and Hardinge looked down at him they did not think at first that he was hurt. He had not cried out and not a muscle of his face had altered. Graham dismounted and knelt down beside him and noticed how composed his features still were; then he saw Moore's left shoulder and was aghast. A round-shot had torn a hole so deep in it that the lung was exposed, the ribs over the heart and part of the collar-bone had been smashed, the muscles of the breast had been torn into strips and the arm was hanging only by the sleeve of his coat and a shred of flesh. The whole of his side was already wet with blood. Hardinge dismounted too and, while Percy, Woodford and Graham galloped off to find a surgeon, Moore took and squeezed his aide-de-camp's hand as he tried to turn to look at the Highlanders. Hardinge reassured him. They were still advancing, he said. And, although Moore did not reply, Hardinge could see from his expression that he was comforted.

A soldier of the 42nd helped to carry the General behind the shelter of a wall and Moore waited there with Hardinge for the surgeon to arrive. The blood was flowing fast from the wound now and Hardinge tried to stem it with his sash; but the hole was too big and Hardinge realised that he must get the General away to a surgeon before he bled to death. He asked him if he would consent to being carried back to the rear. Moore agreed and Hardinge, helped by some Highlanders, lifted him up in a blanket. As they did so, his sword which was hanging on his wounded side touched his arm and became entangled between his legs. Hardinge was unbuckling it when he heard Moore say, in his usual tone and manner and in a very distinct voice, 'It is as well as it is. I had rather it should go out of the field with me.' The General was so calm and composed that Hardinge began to hope that perhaps his wound was not so bad as it appeared, and he tried to comfort him with the suggestion that when the surgeon had dressed his shoulder he would recover. Moore then turned his head round and looked closely at the wound for a few seconds. 'No, Hardinge,' he said decisively, 'I feel that to be impossible.'

The soldiers lifted up the already blood-soaked blanket and put the poles to which its corners were tied over their shoulders. Then they began to walk back with their burden towards Corunna. Hardinge wanted to go with them, but Moore prevented him. 'You need not go with me', he said. 'Report to General Hope that I am wounded, and carried to the rear.' So Hardinge left a sergeant of the 42nd in command of the small party and rode away.

The soldiers carried the General slowly so as not to jolt his arm and several times he made them stop and turn him round to face the front so that he could listen to the firing. It seemed to be growing fainter and he sank back relieved. As the slow procession reached the Santa Lucia road two breathless surgeons hurried up and looked into the blanket. They had been dressing Sir David Baird's arm, which was soon to be cut off at the shoulder, when a message reached the ill-tempered old soldier that the Commander-in-Chief had been badly wounded too. Instantly Baird told the surgeons to stop fussing over him and go to Moore. Sir David was not a man to argue with and they left him in the care of an orderly. But Moore did not want them either. 'You can be of no service to me', he told them when they offered him their services. 'Go to the soldiers to whom you may be useful.'

Moore was right. He had not long to live. Surgeon McGill of the Royals looked into the gaping wound. He took out a piece of cloth and two buttons but could do no more. It was 'quite a hopeless case'.

On the outskirts of Corunna a wagon overtook the party of Highlanders and Colonel Wynch of the 4th, lying wounded in the wagon, asked whom they were carrying in the blanket. When he was told, he suggested that the General should be placed in the wagon too. Moore asked the soldiers if they thought he would be better to move or to stay in the blanket. The blanket would not shake him so much, one of the soldiers replied, as he and the others would 'keep the step and carry him easy'. Moore said, 'I think so too'. And so they went on their way up the road. When they got back to the General's lodgings, an officer noticed, they all had tears in their eyes.

In the hall, François met them. He had been upstairs finishing his master's packing and came down with a candle in his hand. He was 'stunned at the spectacle. But Sir John said to him smiling, "My friend, this is nothing."'

They laid him down on a mattress on the floor and Colonel Anderson went into the room to sit with him. He was in great pain now and when a surgeon examined his wound he could scarcely speak. He felt for Anderson's hand and squeezed it tightly and said, 'Anderson, don't leave me.'

After a little time the spasm passed and he said, 'You know, Anderson, I have always wished to die this way.'

Then he asked him, 'Are the French beaten?' And every time the door opened he looked up and asked the same question in a hoarse and anxious voice: 'Are the French beaten?'

In the valley below the Mero ridge the fight still went on. As the remains of the 42nd Regiment, turned about by Moore's stern words, approached Elvina for the second time that day, Mermet's reserves poured down into the village from the south and Reynaud's brigade from Merle's division approached it from the east. To check this movement, which the men of the 42nd armed only with their bayonets could not resist, Brigadier-General Manningham sent forward his two right-hand regiments, the 3rd Battalion of the 1st and the 2nd Battalion of the 81st. The forces clashed on the gorse and rock-covered ridges of the lower slopes and fought with bitter fury. The 81st lost 150 men, the 1st almost as many. When their ammunition was running low, Hope sent down the reserve regiment from Leith's brigade, the 2nd/ 59th and as darkness fell the French retired.

Further to the east, the village of Piedralonga had also been the scene of bitter fighting. At the beginning of the battle, Delaborde had been content to make those diversionary attacks against Hill's strong positions overlooking the Burgo's tidal estuary which Moore had seen and understood. But in the half-light of the late afternoon General Foy's *voltigeurs* had swooped out of Palavea Abaxo and driven the outposts of Colonel Nicholls's 14th Regiment out of Piedralonga. Hill reacted quickly. Bringing up two companies of the 92nd from the reserve to support the 14th, he gave orders for Colonel Nicholls to retake the village.

It was dusk as the men of the 14th re-entered Palavea Abaxo and they picked their way with difficulty over the broken walls. In the gathering darkness they rushed at the houses which the *voltigeurs* had occupied and tumbled them out at bayonet point. The French troops rallied, however, in a group of grey, decaying houses at the southern end of the village and Delaborde sent forward a battalion to support them there. When night fell, the British held the north and the French the south of the village and the dusty street that ran through it was a silent, dangerous, no-man's land.

All over the field, now, a quiet was descending as the hot guns and muskets cooled in the dark of the early evening. In Elvina the bodies lay in the streets and the helpless wounded cried for water in the scarred houses. To the west Paget's men waited beneath the silent Penasquedo battery for orders to storm it which never came. And farther away to the north, beyond the Heights of San Cristobal, Franceski's cavalrymen were trotting back towards the village of Mesocio, having come up against Fraser's fresh division firmly entrenched on the ridge of Santa Margarita and straddling the road which led across the narrow neck of land and down through Santa Lucia into Corunna.

Hope considered his duty done. The army had fought Soult to a standstill and had gained a short respite. It might now get away on the next day's tide into the open sea. The knowledge that Soult's ammunition must be nearly exhausted, and the sight of the Mero in full tide behind the French army, tempted some officers to suggest to Hope that he should exploit the near-success by sending the reserve with Fraser's division into a new attack. But he refused to risk the chance of being beaten by an army with so much strength in reserve. He had lost between 800 and 900 men, and, although the French had lost rather more, thousands of other French troops would soon be across the Mero. Moore would not, he thought, have wanted him to open a new attack and this, for Hope, was all that mattered.

Behind the white walls of the small house in Corunna, Hope's paragon was dying. He was in terrible pain and asked now and then to be placed in an easier position. But there was no relief. 'I hope the people of England will be satisfied', he said in a brief moment of bitter pride. 'I hope my country will do me justice.'

'Anderson', he said a moment later in a faltering voice. 'You will see my friends as soon as you can. Tell them – everything. Say to my mother . . .' But his strength failed him and he could not finish. He became suddenly agitated. 'Hope – Hope – I have much to say to him, but cannot get it out. Are Colonel Graham and all my aides-de-camp well?'

Anderson turned round and with a quick shake of his head warned those behind him not to say that one of them, Sir Harry Burrard's son, was seriously wounded.

The weak voice spoke again. 'I have made my will, and have remembered my servants. Colborne has my will – and all my papers.'

At that moment Colborne himself came into the room and Moore said to Anderson, 'Remember you go to Willoughby Gordon and tell him it is my request and that I expect he will give Major Colborne a lieutenant-colonelcy. He has long been with me – and I know him most worthy of it.' Then he turned to Colborne and asked again, 'Are the French beaten?' Colborne said that they were, on every point.

'It's a great satisfaction for me,' Moore said and, looking around him, 'Is Paget in the room?'

'No', said Anderson.

'Remember me to him', Moore said in a firmer voice. 'It's General Paget I mean. He is a fine fellow – I feel myself so strong,' he added after a pause as if in apology, 'I fear I shall be long dying.'

There was another pause and when he spoke again, the agony had returned. For the first time he referred to it. 'It is great uneasiness', he murmured. 'It is great pain.'

His mind began to wander. 'Everything François says – is right', he whispered, seeming to search for more coherent words, his face a deadly white. 'I have great confidence in him.'

As he thanked the surgeons again for all the trouble they had taken, Captain Percy came into the room with Charles Stanhope's brother James who had arrived from England a few days before. Moore asked them for news of his other aides-de-camp. Percy said they were all right, and Moore sank back again and for a moment closed his eyes. When he opened them, he saw James Stanhope looking at him piteously.

'Stanhope,' he said, 'remember me to your sister.'

They were the last words he spoke. He pressed Colonel Anderson's hand close to his body and died without a struggle.

Stanhope pushed his way out of the room, his eyes full of tears, and went back towards the front in a kind of bitter fury. He found his fellow aide-de-camp George Napier and suggested to him that they ride together to the 50th Regiment to ask about their brothers. Napier found Charles Stanhope's body being carried off the field, the handsome face covered by a handkerchief, and was able to spare James the shock of discovery; but he could not find his own brother. For hours he went from body to body amidst the gorse and the rocks, along the lines of the olive trees and the aloe hedges, inspecting the features of the dead by the light of a resin torch, until he gave up in despair and returned to his duties with General Hope.

Charles Napier was not dead though. He was lying on a bed of straw in a farmhouse, a prisoner in agony from several wounds. He had been taken as he limped back on his shattered ankle through Elvina with three of his own men from the 50th and an Irishman from the 42nd. In trying to break through to their own lines, all his companions had been killed and he himself had been stabbed in the back by an Italian. Other soldiers had clubbed him with their muskets and one had cut open his head with a brass-hilted sabre before jumping on him, tearing his breeches open and snatching his watch and purse from his pocket. They would have killed him had not a French drummer intervened to save him and helped him away up the lane out of Elvina. In the lane he was almost killed again by one of his own men, a wild and rude Irishman, who not long before had received fifteen hundred lashes for pretending that he had lost the use of his limbs from rheumatism. This intractable soldier came running down towards him, pointing his musket uncertainly at his captors' heads.

'For God's sake, don't fire, Hennessy!' Napier shouted. 'I'm a prisoner and badly wounded and can't help you. Surrender!'

'Surrender! Why should I surrender?' Private Hennessy shouted back in his scarcely intelligible brogue.

'Because there are at least twenty men upon you.'

'Well if I must surrender, there! There's my firelock for you', and he thrust his musket hard at the soldiers' legs and made them jump out of the way clutching their shinbones.

'Stand away ye bloody spalpeens', he roared at them, pushing two of them so hard that they reeled back against a wall.

'I'll carry him myself. Bad luck to the whole bloody lot of ye.'

And so, with indignant pride and disrespectful curses, he helped his major up the lane to captivity in the farmhouse where all night long Napier lay, in agony and despair, believing still that the battle had been lost and that he had helped to lose it.

But two miles away to the north, beyond the rearguard's fires on the deserted hills, the unmolested embarkation which the battle had been fought to secure was going on. Directing the operation, General Hope, fresh from the battlefield, 'looking wild with grief for the loss of his friend, charged through the streets like mad, issuing orders right and left' to the troops filing down wearily to the harbour. Flaring torches lit their way through the streets; and as the tired, smoke-blackened faces passed the uncertain, hissing light, the Spaniards looked out at them from doorways and windows and crossed themselves in fear and pity.

The waters of the harbour were covered by a thick mist through which the men could see but dimly the flickering gleams of the lighthouse and a faint glow from a burning house on the waterfront. The only clear sounds they heard as they were rowed towards the waiting ships were the splash of the oars in the water and the occasional boom of the great French mortars beyond the outposts' fires.

15

The Homecoming

'You know, FitzRoy, we'd not have won, I think, without him.'
The Duke of Wellington

ALL NIGHT LONG the men of the rearguard had kept the fires burning on the hills and had taken turns in running in and out of the light of the flames to give the impression of restless activity. And all night long the sailors had been rowing backwards and forwards between the ships and the harbour wall.

By morning the wounded and more than half the rest of the army were safely aboard the fleet where 'many fell asleep immediately and never awoke for three days and nights'. It had been so misty a night, though, that the sailors had found it impossible to find the ships to which their respective cargoes had been allocated and had put the soldiers and stores aboard the first ship that loomed out of the darkness. On General Leith's ship were the fragments of six different regiments; on another, men from fourteen units were crammed between the decks. In the gathering light of the early morning the embarkation continued. A strong south-westerly wind had sprung up and sprays of surf from the scudding waves were sent flying over the rocks.

On the high ground above them, close to the ramparts of the citadel, a party of men from the 9th Regiment had dug a grave. Moore had told Colonel Anderson that he had always wished to be buried where he had fallen and the previous evening he had asked to be laid next to Brigadier-General Anstruther who had died of exhaustion two days before. General Hope had given orders for this to be done.

At eight o'clock fire was heard beyond the Heights of Santa Margarita and the chaplain was told to begin his service immediately in case the staff should be called away. Followed by Anderson, Colborne, Stanhope and Percy, he led the way to the side of the grave and read a few brief prayers, his voice scarcely audible above the rushing of the wind, the leaves of the prayer book fluttering beneath his fingers.

Moore's body, wrapped in blankets and a military cloak, was lowered into the grave by the red sashes of his staff.

For the rest of that day the embarkation went on, and by nightfall the whole of the army, with the exception of Beresford's brigade of Fraser's division, was aboard the fleet. Beresford had been left to cover the withdrawal and to hand over to General Alcedo who was to do his best to defend the town until the English were at sea. On the morning of the 18th Beresford's brigade began to embark when suddenly from the heights above Fort San Diego there was 'a sudden terrific outburst of fire and it seemed' to Commissary Schaumann, who had just thankfully reached the water's edge, 'as if the Day of Judgment had come'.

> Shot and shell whistled about our heads, and striking first the water, then the sloops, and anon the ships themselves, made hearing and seeing almost impossible. It was the French who at this very moment had opened fire from their batteries in order to shell and bombard the harbour and the fleet.

One of the soldiers near him, outraged by this last attempt of the French to prevent him reaching home when he was so nearly there, ground his teeth in fury and then, suddenly turning round, shook his fist at the battery and in a voice of such comical exasperation that his companions could not help laughing, shouted out 'Ah, you mad, mad beasts'.

The sloops at which he had just been looking with satisfaction could not come up close to the shore, but had to be kept at a safe distance from the rocks by means of their oars. The soldiers had to clamber to the edge of the rocks which were being washed by the surf and then, with the water splashing over them, take hold of the oars held out to them in the strong grips of the sailors. They were then seized by the sailors and dragged on to the boats like turtles. The naval officer in command of the sloops shouted that only men could be got aboard and 'swore like mad' when anyone tried to get luggage into the boats, throwing valises and bags overboard with indiscriminate anger. Schaumann's valise, containing everything that he had, was being snatched from his hands by the furious officer when the enterprising commissary clutched it to his breast defiantly and cried out, 'I am a commissary, and this valise contains public papers and money'.

'Well then, stick to it and be damned', shouted the officer almost beside himself with rage.

For nearly an hour the bombardment continued. But although the damage done to the shipping was negligible – only one boat was overturned, drowning nine men of the Royal Wagon Train – the masters of several vessels cut their cables and allowed their craft to run ashore in the strong wind. 'It is only wonderful', Captain Boothby told his brother, that more did not strike upon the leeward rocks. Seven, I believe, struck, three were got off, and four, after being cleared, were burnt by us, and beautifully lighted the last of the embarkation. The transports that were got off had been previously abandoned by their masters.

A midshipman of the *Barfleur* told me that on going alongside of a transport on the rocks, the master threw his trunk into the boat, jumped in after it, and then, before a single soldier was out, he cried, 'Shove off, or she'll bilge'. He was shoved backwards by a sailor.

In Corunna the excitement was chaotic. 'The enthusiastic blaze in the good cause continued to increase', Boothby's account continued. 'Everybody commanded, everybody fired, everybody hallooed, everybody ordered silence, everybody forbade the fire, everybody thought musketry best, and everybody cannon.' Women ran up to the batteries with cartridges and wads for the cannon on their heads. Some stayed there with their men and swore that they would die with them rather than let the French pass through the walls, which they were so anxious to defend unaided that orders had been given that the British rearguard should not appear on them. Other women rushed back to the shore and stood on the rocks to wave goodbye as the fleet sailed out to sea.

It was a rough and uncomfortable passage home. The small transports were crammed to the bulwarks with filthy, blood-smeared soldiers; with terrified horses that stamped and kicked viciously in holds so tightly packed that they could only move their legs; with guns and baggage and rows of wounded men with maggots crawling in their wounds beneath slimy bandages.

In the Bay of Biscay a gale blew, dispersing the convoy over hundreds of miles of sea and sending the small, laden transports scudding through the foam-lashed waters. On the 22nd the wind dropped, but three days later it had risen again, sending the *Dispatch* and *Smallbridge* crashing on to the Cornish rocks with the loss of 273 men of the 7th Hussars and the King's German Legion.

Between January 29th and 31st, at nearly every port along the coast between Falmouth and Dover, the creaking vessels came in to land their shocking cargoes. Ragged, bearded, caked in dirt and covered with lice the soldiers stumbled up the quay sides. Harry Smith of the Rifle Brigade went into the George Inn where a colonel roared at his thin white face, 'Who the devil's ghost are you?' Some soldiers, ashamed of their appearance, like a gallant sergeant of the 43rd, were 'glad to escape observation and march quickly into barracks' where their insect-ridden clothes 'far too bad for amendment were speedily burned'. Others, wily old soldiers, well aware of the advantages to be gained by it, 'recited in pathetic strain the most frightful accounts of their sufferings and hardships'. Many men had contracted typhus on the voyage home, and soon the hospitals in all the ports were full to overflowing, and store-ships and even prison-ships became crowded with the sick.

The news of the horrifying return of these filthy, ill and cadaverous soldiers spread fast through an indignant country. 'The fact must not be disguised,' wrote a correspondent to *The Times,* expressing a general opinion, 'that we have suffered a shameful disaster.' It was all very well to talk of the courage and endurance of the troops but of what use were these virtues alone when pitted against the genius of Napoleon? 35,000 men had crossed the Spanish frontier against him; 8,000 had not returned. We were unworthy of our great past. 'We can only fight', said Walter Scott, indignantly ashamed, 'like mastiffs, blindly and desperately.'

Despite his hero's death, Sir John Moore himself was widely blamed. While Marshal Soult gave orders for the erection of a monument in Corunna, the Government in London did little to defend his reputation against those critics, both in Parliament and outside it, who were intent on blackening it. Unaware of the reasons which lay behind his actions, soldiers and civilians alike condemned them. He had placed his army in an impossible situation and then, after days of uncertainty and vacillation, had been chased half way across Spain ignoring every position of strength at which he might have turned and fought back successfully. Destroying the army by his wild, precipitate retreat he had become obsessed by his overwhelming anxiety to reach the sea. One of his own young officers and bitterest critics afterwards wrote:

> Sir John Moore proved lamentably deficient in those qualities of decision and firmness which he had so often displayed on former occasions, and which alone would have enabled him to extricate the army by some brilliant achievement, from the perilous situation in which it had been placed by his own ill-advised measures and the disasters of our Spanish allies. At this juncture, however, he appeared to labour under a depression of spirits so different from his usual serene and cheerful disposition as to give a mournful expression to his countenance, indicative of the greatest anxiety of mind; and it seemed either that his judgment was completely clouded or that he was under the influence of a spell which forced him to commit the most glaring errors.

Throughout the winter the memory of Moore, the Army which he had helped to train and the invidious Spanish people whom England had tried to save, were all under constant and indiscriminate attack. News of further Spanish military disasters and the crowning of Joseph Buonaparte in Madrid gave an unhealthy satisfaction to the pessimists, while the well-publicised revelation that a former mistress of the Duke of York had been using her influence to deal in Army commissions and promotions on an enormous scale gave not only pleasure to a scandal-loving public but invaluable material to those for whom the Army was both a threat to the reputation of the country and a sink of corruption.

But the very violence of the critics and of the parliamentary opposition; their complete failure to agree on a common policy or reasonable targets; their extravagant attacks, so easily impugned as both hysterical and treacherous, soon condemned them. By the early spring the mood of the country had changed. Lord Grenville's contention that Corunna had proved that an English army must never set foot on the continent again, did not make sense to a country which felt its honour was at stake. 'If Napoleon has trounced us, which I don't believe,' a clergyman in Leicester wrote to his sister, 'we must trounce him back.' On April 15th Sir Arthur Wellesley sailed for Portugal again with that intention in mind.

The Austrians under the Archduke Charles had marched across the Inn a week before, announcing their determination to liberate the German people from their French oppressors. The Spanish people too had risen once more in what promised this time to be a successful revolt. Napoleon's contemptuous treatment of their national dignity and his army's ruthless exploitation of their poor countryside had driven thousands of peasants into the hills, where they formed bands of revengeful *guerrilleros* and fell down on French outposts and wagon trains with ferocious cruelty. Soult's divisions and then Ney's had trampled over Galicia after Moore's withdrawal at Corunna, and the people had turned on them in fury. And, because Moore had dragged them away into the bleak remote provinces of the north, the south of Spain was still free. Seville remained in Spanish hands; Cadiz was still open to British shipping. With the power of the Navy to support him freely, Wellesley landed at Lisbon with hope and confidence.

Others might belittle Moore's achievements; Wellesley did not. He thought his conduct of the past campaign skilful and imaginative, and he knew how much he owed to it. At the beginning of May he advanced north against Soult on the Douro and in a magnificent, dangerous attack across a river in full flood threw him back towards Spain. It was the beginning of a long and bitter struggle but it was the advent too of victory.

Four years later his army marched from its victory at Vitoria towards the long line of the Pyrenees and then across towards the sea and through the burning ruins of San Sebastian. The French were driven back, still fighting, towards Biarritz and the Peninsular War was over. Riding over the frontier Lord Wellington grumbled at his army with familiar disgust. They were a set of drunken brutes, the scum of the earth. But there were those who recognised beneath the often repeated words, beyond the irritation of fatigue, rheumatism and lumbago, behind the patrician scorn, an unwilling affection and respect. Years later he admitted it: 'I could have done *anything* with that army. It was in such splendid order.'

And he did not forget, nor ever forgot, the man who had done so much to make it so. As an old man at the Horse Guards he said one day to his Military Secretary, the future Lord Raglan, 'You know, FitzRoy, we'd not have won, I think, without him.' For the regiments that Moore had so finely trained were 'the backbone of the Army'.

APPENDIX I

Composition of British Forces

(The figures in brackets indicate the number of men lost during the campaign)

BAIRD'S DIVISION

WARDE'S BRIGADE
1st Btn, 1st Foot Guards (74)
2nd Btn, 1st Foot Guards (66)

BENTINCK'S BRIGADE
1st Btn, 4th Regiment (149)
1st Btn, 42nd Regiment (161)
1st Btn, 50th Regiment (264)

MANNINGHAM'S BRIGADE
3rd Btn, 1st Regiment (216)
1st Btn, 26th Regiment (208)
1st Btn, 81st Regiment (241)

HOPE'S DIVISION

LEITH'S BRIGADE
51st Regiment (107)
2nd Btn, 59th Regiment (143)
76th Regiment (170)

HILL'S BRIGADE
2nd Regiment (205)
1st Btn, 5th Regiment (239)
2nd Btn, 14th Regiment (138)
1st Btn, 32nd Regiment (187)

CATLIN CRAWFURD'S BRIGADE
1st Btn, 36th Regiment (243)
1st Btn, 71st Regiment (138)
1st Btn, 92nd Regiment (129)

FRASER'S DIVISION

BERESFORD'S BRIGADE
1st Btn, 6th Regiment (391)
1st Btn, 9th Regiment (373)
2nd Btn, 23rd Regiment (172)
2nd Btn, 43rd Regiment (230)

FANE'S BRIGADE
1st Btn, 38th Regiment (143)
1st Btn, 79th Regiment (155)
Ist Btn, 82nd Regiment (228)

EDWARD PAGET'S RESERVE DIVISION

ANSTRUTHER'S BRIGADE
20th Regiment (113)
1st Btn, 52nd Regiment (143)
1st Btn, 95th Regiment (157)

DISNEY'S BRIGADE
1st Btn, 28th Regiment (302)
1st Btn, 91st Regiment (212)

THE LIGHT BRIGADES

ROBERT CRAUFURD'S
1ST LIGHT BRIGADE
1st Btn, 43rd Regiment (85)
2nd Btn, 52nd Regiment (161)
2nd Btn, 95th Regiment (96)

KARL ALTEN'S 2ND LIGHT
BRIGADE
1st Light Btn, King's German
Legion (163 – including 22 men
drowned on the voyage home)
2nd Light Btn, King's German
Legion (262 – including 187 men
drowned on the voyage home)

LORD PAGET'S CAVALRY DIVISION

18th Light Dragoons (77)
3rd Light Dragoons, King's German Legion (56)
7th Hussars★ (97 – including 56 men drowned
on the voyage home)
10th Hussars (24)
15th Hussars (24)

★ The Hussar regiments were more correctly known as Light Dragoons until the end of
the Napoleonic Wars and were listed as such in the Army Lists. Napier calls the 15th,
Light Dragoons but the 7th, 10th and 18th, Hussars. Fortescue shows them all as Light
Dragoons. I have followed Oman whose titles were, it seems, acceptable to
contemporaries.

APPENDIX II

Changes in Regimental Titles

Original number until 1881	County Affiliation or Other Title, as at 1809	Title 1881–1957	Present Title
1st	The Royal Regiment	Royal Scots	Royal Scots
2nd	Queen's Royal Regiment	Queen's Royal Regiment	Queen's Surrey Regiment (on amalgamation with East Surreys)
4th	King's Own Regiment	King's Own Royal Regiment	King's Own Border Regiment (on amalgamation with Border Regiment)
5th	Northumberland Regiment	Royal Northumberland Fusiliers	Royal Northumberland Fusiliers
6th	First Warwickshire Regiment	Royal Warwickshire Regiment	Royal Warwickshire Regiment
9th	East Norfolk Regiment	Royal Norfolk Regiment	1st East Anglian Regiment (on amalgamation with Suffolk Regiment)
14th	Buckinghamshire Regiment	West Yorkshire Regiment	Prince of Wales's Own Regiment of Yorkshire (on amalgamation with East Yorkshire Regiment)
20th	East Devonshire Regiment	Lancashire Fusiliers	Lancashire Fusiliers
23rd	Royal Welch Fusiliers	Royal Welch Fusiliers	Royal Welch Fusiliers
26th	Cameronians	Cameronians	Cameronians
28th	North Gloucestershire Regiment	Gloucestershire Regiment	Gloucestershire Regiment
32nd	Cornwall Regiment	Duke of Cornwall's Light Infantry	Somerset and Cornwall Light Infantry (on amalgamation with Somerset Light Infantry)
36th	Herefordshire Regiment	Worcestershire Regiment	Worcestershire Regiment

Original num- ber until 1881	County Affiliation or Other Title, as at 1809	Title 1881–1957	Present Title
38th	First Staffordshire Regiment	South Staffordshire Regiment	Staffordshire Regiment (on amalgamation with North Staffordshire Regiment)
42nd	Royal Highland Regiment	Black Watch	Black Watch
43rd	Monmouthshire Regiment	Oxfordshire and Buckinghamshire Light Infantry	1st Greenjackets
50th	Queen's Own Regiment	Royal West Kent Regiment	Queen's Own Buffs (on amalgamation with the Buffs)
51st	2nd Yorkshire, West Riding Regiment or The King's Own Light Infantry	King's Own Yorkshire Light Infantry	King's Own Yorkshire Light Infantry
52nd	Oxfordshire Regiment	Oxfordshire and Buckinghamshire Light Infantry	1st Greenjackets
59th	2nd Nottinghamshire Regiment	East Lancashire Regiment	Lancashire Regiment (on amalgamation with South Lancashire Regiment)
71st	Highlanders	Highland Light Infantry	Royal Highland Fusiliers (on amalgamation with Royal Scots Fusiliers)
76th	–	Duke of Wellington's Regiment	Duke of Wellington's Regiment
79th	Cameron Highlanders	Cameron Highlanders	Queen's Own Highlanders (on amalgamation with Seaforth Highlanders)
81st	–	Loyal Regiment	Loyal Regiment
82nd	The Prince of Wales's Volunteers	South Lancashire Regiment	Lancashire Regiment (on amalgamation with East Lancashire Regiment)
91st	–	Argyll & Sutherland Highlanders	Argyll & Sutherland Highlanders
92nd	–	Gordon Highlanders	Gordon Highlanders
95th	The 95th Regiment became the Rifle Brigade in 1815 when its number was re-allotted to an ordinary line battalion which had the county affiliation of Derbyshire and which later became the 2nd Btn, The Sherwood Foresters.		
7th Hussars	–	7th Hussars	The Queen's Hussars (on amalgamation with the 3rd Hussars)

Original number until 1881	County Affiliation or Other Title, as at 1809	Title 1881–1957	Present Title
10th Hussars	–	10th Hussars or The Prince of Wales's Own Royal Regiment of Light Dragoons	10th Hussars
15th Hussars	–	1st Hussars or the King's Light Dragoons	15/19th King's Royal Hussars (on amalgamation in 1922 with 19th Hussars)
18th Light Dragoons	–	18th Hussars or 18th Light Dragoons	13/18th Royal Hussars (on amalgamation in 1922 with 13th Hussars)

A Note on Sources

In an interesting letter dated 20 July, 1902, which is stuck between the leaves of the first volume of one of the London Library's copies of his *History of the Peninsular War,* Sir Charles Oman admits to Paget Toynbee that he has 'been rather hard, perhaps, on Moore. One does not allow enough for the difficulties of a British general of those days, set to handle a large body of men unaccustomed to act in masses, or to move in an unknown district. But Napier makes him so impeccable, that the spots on the sun attract more attention than they deserve perhaps!'

The first volume of General Napier's great history had been published in 1828. Napier had been induced to write it by a determination to save the reputation of Sir John Moore from further attacks by Tory writers. Already Robert Southey had produced the first volume of his *History of the Peninsular War;* and it was partly with a view to correcting what he took to be Southey's misrepresentations that Napier set to work.

He was not, at first, successful. The sales of his book so disappointed his publisher, John Murray, that the remaining volumes were published at the author's own expense. As each successive volume appeared, however, the fame of the book grew and when completed it was universally recognised as one of the finest military histories ever written.

Before the last volume was published other writers had entered the field. In 1829 General Charles Stewart brought out an account of the campaign which was so critical of Moore that Dr. James Moore, Sir John's brother, decided to take up his pen again. In the year of his brother's death he had published *A Narrative of the Campaign of the British Army in Spain* based on official documents and dispatches; now James Moore published in three volumes *The Life of Lieutenant-General Sir John Moore* which appeared in 1834.

Numerous memoirs and biographies – both reliable and misleading – were also published at this time by officers and men who disagreed as violently about Moore as the historians did. To some he was a gloomy, irresolute man who had destroyed his army by a wild rush at a vastly superior enemy, followed by a headlong scramble out of the trap into which Napoleon had enticed him; to others he was a brilliant hero who, outnumbered ten to one, had skilfully used a tiny army to draw the French into northern Spain and by defeating them there had ensured that their plans to seize Portugal and Andalusia had to be abandoned.

In the second half of the nineteenth century the controversy died down, to be revived by Sir Charles Oman. While recognising that Napier was a wonderfully eloquent writer, Oman found him prejudiced and on occasions 'unfortunately quite inaccurate'. Sir Charles, himself, cannot be entirely acquitted of this latter charge, although in a book which runs to 4,543 pages and is a mass of laboriously collected detail it is no doubt churlish to find minor faults.

His opinions, however, could not be so readily excused by Moore's admirers. And one of these immediately leapt to the general's defence. Major-General Sir J. F. Maurice edited Moore's journal and presented it to the public with a long commentary in 1904. In this, while making several irrefutable criticisms of Oman's strictures, Maurice went so far as to suggest that the Corunna campaign was the 'boldest, the most successful, the most brilliant stroke of war of all time'. This extravagant panegyric was followed by the sixth volume of the Hon. John Fortescue's *History of the British Army* in which Moore's services although more cautiously assessed are highly regarded.

In recent years Sir Arthur Bryant, Major-General J. F. C. Fuller and Miss Carola Oman have combined to ensure that this justifiably approving assessment cannot seriously be questioned again. I have included in the bibliography some books, mainly diaries and memoirs of soldiers, which do not deal specifically with the Corunna campaign.

I have added them to the list because I have made use of them in describing scenes and personalities which those immediately involved have not described so well.

I have not found any manuscript sources which add anything of interest to what has been published. The papers in the Public Record Office, however, contain the full text of various orders and despatches which have not been printed in full for fear of causing offence to people mentioned in them still living at the time of publication.

Bibliography

ANDERSON, J. A., *Recollections of a Peninsular Veteran*, 1913
ANTON, James, *Retrospect of a Military Life*, 1841
The Autobiography and Services of Sir James McGrigor, Bart, 1861
The autobiography of Lieutenant General Sir Harry Smith, Vol. I, 1902
The autobiography of Sergeant William Laurence, 1901
BALAGNY, D. E. P., *Campagne de l'Empereur Napoléon en Espagne 1808–1809*, Five Volumes, 1902
BEAMISH, N. L., *History of the King's German Legion*, 1832
BELL, G., *Rough notes by an old soldier*, 1867
BELMAS, J., *Précis Historique de la guerre de la Péninsule*, 1836
BOTELHO, J. J. Teixeira, *Guerra del Península*, 1915
BRADFORD, William, *Sketches of the Country Character and Costume in Portugal and Spain*, 1809
BRETT JAMES, Antony, *General Graham, Lord Lynedoch*, 1959
BROWNRIGG, Beatrice, *Life and Letters of Sir John Moore*, 1823
BRYANT, Arthur, *The Years of Victory*, 1944
BRUCE, H. A. (Editor), *Life of General Sir William Napier*, Vol. I, 1864
BURNE, A. H., *The Noble Duke of York*, 1950
CADELL, Lieutenant-Colonel Charles, *Narrative of the Campaigns of the 28th Regiment*, 1835
CARR-GOMM, F. C. (Editor), *Letters and Journals of Field-Marshal Sir William Maynard Gomm from 1799 to Waterloo 1815*, 1881
du CASSE (Editor), *Correspondance de Napoléon I*, 1887
CHARMILLY, Colonel Venault de, *Narrative of his transactions in Spain with the Rt. Hon. John Hookham Frere*, 1810
The Confidential Correspondence of Napoleon Buonaparte, 1855
COPE, Sir William Henry, *The History of the Rifle Brigade*, 1877
Correspondence, Despatches and other Papers of Viscount Castlereagh, Vol. V, 2nd series, 1851
COSTELLO, Edward, *The Adventures of a Soldier*, 1841
CURLING, Henry (Editor), *Recollections of Rifleman Harris*, 1848
DELAVOYE, A. M., *Life of Thomas Graham, Lord Lynedoch*, 1880
The Diary of William Gavin, 1815
DONALDSON, J., *The Eventful Life of a Soldier during the Late War in Spain, Portugal and France*, 1827
FESTING, Gabriel, *John Hookham Frere and his friends*, 1899
FORTESCUE, The Hon. J. W., *History of the British Army*, Vol. VI, 2nd Edition, 1921
FOY, Le Général, *Histoire de la guerre de la Péninsule*, 1828
FULLER, Major-General J. F. C., *Sir John Moore's System of Training*, 1925
GARDYNE, A. D. G., *The Life of a Regiment*, 1901
Gaceta de Madrid
The Gentleman's Magazine

GIROD de l'AIN, Maurice, *Vie Militaire du Général Foy,* 1900

GLEIG, Rev. R. (Editor), *The Hussar. The Story of Nobert Landsheit*

GOMEZ, DE ARTECHE Y MORO, Jose, *Geografia historico–militar de España y Portugal,* 1859

GRASSETT, A., *La Guerre d'Espagne, 1807–1813,* 1914

GRATTAN, W., *Adventures with the Connaught Rangers,* 1847

HAMILTON, Thomas, *Annals of the Peninsular Campaigns,* 1829

HASLIP, Joan, *Lady Hester Stanhope,* 1934

HENNEGAY, Sir Richard, *Seven Years Campaigning in the Peninsula and the Netherlands,* 1846

HYLTON, Lord (Editor), *The Paget Brothers,* 1918

ILCHESTER, The Earl of (Editor), *The Spanish Journal of Elizabeth Lady Holland,* 1910

Jottings from My Sabretasch by a Chelsea Pensioner, 1847

Journal du Général Fantin des Odoards, 1895

Journal of the Royal Army Medical Corps

Journal of the Royal Artillery

Journal of the Royal United Service Institution

Journal of the Society for Army Historical Research

Journal of Sergeant D. Robertson, 1842

Journal of A Soldier of the Seventy-First Regiment, Highland Light Infantry, from 1806 to 1815, 1822

KINCAID, John, *Adventures in the Rifle Brigade,* 1830

Random shots from a Rifleman, 1835

LAWRENCE, Rosamund, *Charles Napier: Friend and Fighter,* 1952

LEACH, Lieutenant-Colonel J., *Rough Sketches of the life of an old soldier,* 1831

LEITH HAY, Sir Andrew, *A Narrative of the Peninsular War,* 1850

LIDDELL HART, Captain B. H. (Editor) *The Letters of Private Wheeler,* 1951

LUDOVICI, Anthony M. (Editor), *On the Road with Wellington. The Diary of August Ludolf Friedrich Schaumann,* 1924

McGUFFIE, T. H., *Peninsular Cavalry General. The Correspondence of Lieutenant-General Robert Ballard Long,* 1951

MAURICE, Major-General Sir J. F. (Editor), *The Diary of Sir John Moore in two volumes,* Vol. II, 1904

MAXWELL, W. H. (Editor), *Peninsular Sketches by Actors on the Scene,* 1848

Memoirs of the Late Lieutenant-General Sir James Leith by a British Officer, 1818

Mémoires Militaires du Maréchal Jourdan, 1859

Memoirs of a Sergeant of the 5th Regiment of Foot

Memoirs of a Sergeant late in the 43rd Regiment during the Peninsular War, 1839

Mémoires sur les Opérations Militaires des Français en Galice, en Portugal, et dans la vallée du Tage en 1809, 1821

MILBURNE, H. R. *A Narrative of the Circumstances attending the retreat of the British Army under Sir John Moore,* 1809

Moniteur

MOORE, James Carrick, *The Life of Lieutenant-General Sir John Moore, Vol. II,* 1834

A Narrative of the Campaign of the British Army in Spain commanded by his Excellency Lieutenant-General Sir John Moore, 1809

MOORE-SMITH, G. C., *Life and Letters of John Colborne, Field-Marshal Lord Seaton,* 1903

MOORSOM, W. S., *History of the 52nd Oxfordshire Light Infantry,* 1860

NAPIER, Sir William, *History of the War in the Peninsula and in the South of France from the year 1807 to the year 1814, Vol. I, Book III,* 1882

The Life and Opinions of General Sir Charles James Napier, Vol. I, 1857

De NAYLIES, *Mémoires sur la Guerre d'Espagne,* 1817

NEALE, Adam, *The Spanish Campaign of 1808*, 1826, (Constable's Miscellany, Vol. XXVII)

OMAN, Carola, *Sir John Moore*, 1953

OMAN, Sir Charles, *A History of the Peninsular War, Vol. I*, 1902
Wellington's Army 1809–1814, 1912

ORMSBY, Rev. J. W., *An Account of the Operations of the British Army in Spain and Portugal during the Campaign of 1808-1809*, Two Volumes, 1809

Oxfordshire Light Infantry Chronicle

PAGET, Sir A. (Editor), *The Paget Papers*, Two Volumes, 1896

PAGET, Eden (Editor), *Letters and Memorials of General the Hon. Sir Edward Paget*, 1898

Parliamentary Papers for 1808 and 1809

Passages in the Early Military Life of General Sir George Napier, written by himself, 1884

PATTERSON, Major, *Leaves from the Journal of a Veteran*, 1845

PORTER, Sir R. Ker, *Letters from Portugal and Spain written during the march of the British troops under Sir John Moore*, 1809

QUEIPO DE LLANO Y RUIZ DE SARAVIA, *Historia del levantamiento, guerra y revolucion de España*, 1835–37

Recollections of the Peninsula, 1825

ROUSSEAU, I. J. (Editor), *The Peninsular Journal of Major-General Sir Benjamin D'Urban*, 1930

Royal Engineers Journal

Royal Military Chronicle

Royal Military Panorama

SADLER, Thomas, *Diary, Reminiscences and Correspondence of Henry Crabb Robinson*, Vol. I, 1869

SORELL, Lieutenant-Colonel T. S., *Notes on the Campaign of 1808–1809 in the North of Spain*, 1828

Souvenirs Militaires du Colonel de Gonneville, 1875

STEEVENS, Lieutenant-Colonel Charles, *Reminiscences of My Military Life from 1795 to 1818*, 1878

STIRLING, Captain James, *Memoirs of the Campaign in 1808 in Spain under Lieutenant-General Sir John Moore*

STURGIS, Julian (Editor), *A Boy in the Peninsular War. The Services, adventures and experience of Robert Blakeney*, 1899

SURTEES, William, *Twenty-five years in the Rifle Brigade*, 1833

The Times

Under England's Flag. The Memoirs, Diary and Correspondence of Charles Boothby, 1900

VANE, General Charles William, Marquess of Londonderry, *Story of the Peninsular War*, 1849

de VILLA-URRUTIA, W. R., *Relaciones entre España é Inglaterra durante la guerra de la independencia*, 1911

VIVIAN, The Hon. Claud, *Richard Hussey Vivian*, 1897

The War in the Peninsula: Some letters of Lieutenant Robert Knowles, 1913

WARRE, Rev. Edmond (Editor), *Letters from the Peninsula 1808–1812 by Lieutenant-General Sir William Warre*, 1909

WHINYATES, Colonel F. A., *From Corunna to Sevastopol. The History of 'C' Battery 'A' Brigade Royal Horse Artillery*, 1884

WYLLY, Colonel H. C. (Editor), *Journal of Captain Gordon of the 15th Hussars*, 1913

Index

The Windrush Press

MILITARY HISTORY BOOKS

THE LETTERS OF PRIVATE WHEELER 1809–1828

An eyewitness account of the Battle of Waterloo
Edited and with a foreward by B. H. Liddell Hart
*'Vivid images – of people, landscape, events – flow from his
pen . . . one of military history's great originals'*
John Keegan
Paperback £9.99

THE DIARY OF A NAPOLEONIC FOOTSOLDIER

Jakob Walter

A conscript in the *Grande Armée's* account of the long march
home on the retreat from Moscow
Edited and Introduced by Mark Raeff
Hardback £11.99 Illustrated

A SOLDIER OF THE SEVENTY-FIRST

The Journal of a Soldier in the Peninsular War
Edited and Introduced by Christopher Hibbert
Paperback £9.99

RECOLLECTIONS OF RIFLEMAN HARRIS

One of the most popular military books of all time.
Edited and Introduced by Christopher Hibbert
Paperback £9.99

The Windrush Press

GREAT BATTLES SERIES

AGINCOURT

Christopher Hibbert
Paperback £9.99 Illustrated

EDGEHILL

Peter Young
Paperback £15.99 Illustrated

CORUNNA

Christopher Hibbert
Paperback £12.99 Illustrated

HASTINGS

Peter Poyntz Wright
Paperback £9.99 Illustrated

WELLINGTON'S PENINSULAR VICTORIES

Michael Glover
Paperback £12.99 Illustrated

Order from THE WINDRUSH PRESS, LITTLE WINDOW, HIGH
STREET, MORETON-IN-MARSH, GLOS. GL56 0LL
MAJOR CREDIT CARDS ACCEPTED
TEL: 01608 652012 FAX: 01608 652125
Free postage within the UK